THE
Paranoid Parents
GUIDE

Worry Less, Parent Better, and Raise a Resilient Child

Christie Barnes

Founder, Paranoid Parents Anonymous

www.paranoidparentsguide.com

Health Communications, Inc.
Deerfield Beach, Florida

www.hcibooks.com

Library of Congress Cataloging-in-Publication Data

Barnes, Christie.
  The paranoid parents guide : worry less, parent better, and raise a resilient
child / Christie Barnes.
    p. cm.
  ISBN-13: 978-0-7573-1505-3
  ISBN-10: 0-7573-1505-4
    1. Parenting.   2. Parents—Psychology.   3. Child rearing.   4. Parent and
child.   5.Resilience (Personality trait) in children.   I. Title.
  HQ755.8.B374 2010
  649'.1—dc22

                                                                   2010021560
©2010 Christie Barnes

HCI, its logos, and its marks are trademarks of Health Communications, Inc.

Publisher: Health Communications, Inc.
            3201 S.W. 15th Street
            Deerfield Beach, FL 33442-8190

Cover design by Larissa Hise Henoch
Inside book design by Lawna Patterson Oldfield
Inside formatting by Dawn Von Strolley Grove

To Peter, Leela, Abby, Nathan, and Zach

Contents

Acknowledgments..vii

Chapter 1   Worrying: The Nation's Hobby of Choice.......1

Chapter 2   Worry Crazy Makers 11

Chapter 3   Why Worry Is Dangerous: The Science
             of the Fear Epidemic 23

Chapter 4   Myths Exposed: Parents' Top Worries
             Versus Children's Real Dangers.....................37

Chapter 5   Age-Group Essentials: Overview..................105

Chapter 6   Infants 111

Chapter 7   Toddlers..121

Chapter 8   Elementary School..143

Chapter 9   Middle School 173

Chapter 10 High School 183

Chapter 11 College 191

Chapter 12 The Recovering Worry Addict.....................199

Statistical Sources 233

Products 249

Index..251

Acknowledgments

"You would tell every parent in the country how to parent their kids if you could," my husband, Peter, said to me.

Little did we dream that I would have the chance to do just that. Actually, I think he half meant that I was being a bossy know-it-all. But little did he know that my viewpoint would be channeled productively into a positive-help book for worried parents like I used to be.

My husband was the writer of some of America's most beloved miniseries and TV movies. And he wrote Oscar-nominated movies. So my book will never reach the mass audiences his work reached. But then, *The Paranoid Parents Guide* won't have million-dollar Super Bowl commercials that his Hallmark ABC miniseries had.

But we both speak to our children through our writing. He died when my children were very young, but he still "speaks" to our children through his work. My writing has made me literally speak to our children differently—better—each day.

After his death, the inspired lawyer Patty Mayer told me I must do something with Paranoid Parents, which I had been researching. And that led to the Paranoid Parents Stop Worrying Shoppe, then to products like the minibook kits that were a hit for Uncommon Goods. Then came the website.

I was discovered by my clever, insightful editor Allison Janse. She has never actually told me she was a paranoid parent, but as a mother of twins, I can guess she worries. Actually, she has said that she keeps my Sanity Cards on her bedside table to keep her concerns in perspective during those awake-worrying nights.

My four children—Leela, Abby, Nathan, and Zach—didn't deserve a paranoid mom. "Our mom's paranoid, you know. But she is getting better," they say.

I am very fortunate to have an extended family of experts in the health business. I couldn't have written this book without the reality checks from my brother, Scott Horn, formerly of the Kitsap County Health Department in Washington State and now physicist and geographer.

My cousin Dr. Nedrow Calonge is the chief medical officer of Colorado overseeing all state public health issues from pandemics to nutrition to bioterrorism. His wife, Susan Calonge, a teacher, wrote Paranoid Parents' *Tantrum Tamers* minibook kit. Cousins Kathleen Hanrahan and her husband Dr. Richard Capek always had unerring advice on what battles to fight for your kids.

My kids' older cousins help me and my kids navigate a "good

kid" path to adulthood: Megan, Dara, Kelly, Cailin, Brendan, Devon, and Taylor.

I thank Heidi Roy, supermom and confessed paranoid parent, who has helped me so much. Linda Petrie Bunch and Tibby Rothman designed a great website for me.

And thanks to all the worried parents out there dedicated to parenting well.

Chapter One

Worrying: The Nation's Hobby of Choice

Is this really the right school? Should I make my kids wear life jackets at the neighborhood pool party? Jimmy's had a cough for a week. Does Amy's mom have enough booster seats for the movie trip? Is my child gifted? We watched more than an hour of TV. Is Bruce's trampoline safe? How could we forget the sight words we practiced this summer? Will my kids get kidnapped at the mall? What about playing with toy guns? Do kids need to wear helmets while riding their bikes in the driveway? Will he have too many activities if we add tae kwon do? Do we need toddler Mandarin classes for Harvard?

What did you worry about today—or in the last fifteen minutes?

If you're like most parents, these seemingly life-or-death worries and critical future-determining decisions probably flash through your mind on a regular basis.

There is a lot to be on top of when you're a parent. Every day some new unexpected problems are thrown our way. Although I am exaggerating how crucial each decision is, sometimes all the decisions seem important, as if there were no going back for your child's well-being and future prosperity if you make even one wrong turn.

An endless podcast of worries plays like audio wallpaper in the back of a parent's mind. Some of us tune into "Worries FM" more than others.

What's Playing on Worries FM?

I worry; therefore I am (a good parent). Whoever worries more loves more. The more sleepless nights I have, the more caring a parent I am.

I used to think that I worried more than any other parent I knew. But everywhere I went, there was always a parent saying, "As a parent you just can't help worrying." At Scouts, by the pool, in the classroom, on vacation, at church, in the grocery store checkout line, at the soccer game, there was always somebody worrying about their kids.

And almost every parent I met insisted that he or she worried more than I did.

The Five-Minute Worry Test

Sit down, take a piece of paper and for five minutes write down the things that you worry about for your child. The list can include dangers, fears, and worries. Then underline what you perceive as the most dangerous or crucial one of all.

In the Paranoid Parents focus groups that I conduct, some parents have easily come up with a list of 125 worries in five minutes. Even worse, some parents can find a potential danger in everything they see: a glass to break, a possibly poison leaf to eat, a sofa to fall off of, a DVD player to stick something in, a pillow to suffocate someone, a bed to jump on, a grape to choke on, a slick floor to slip on, a Wii nun chuck cord to getting strangled with.

In our focus groups, most parents described themselves as "worried parents." About 75 percent of parents who were polled either started or ended their five-minute worry test with the word *everything*. "I worry about everything," they freely admitted. Ironically, the 25 percent of parents who said they felt in control were no better off than the paranoid set because they were *completely wrong* about what the serious dangers were for their kids. In other words, they're *not* worrying about the things they *should* worry about.

Most parents worry. Even worse, in most cases their top-ten dangers are sensational tragedies they are powerless to control. The odds of any one of these catastrophes happening to a child are 1 in 10 million, but they are the dangers that parents worry about most.

How long was your list? What was on it?

How a Paranoid Parent's
Life Became a Campaign

I first realized that I worried a lot when I was pregnant with triplets. The scene was a Sunday outing to a park with friends, my husband, and our two-and-a-half-year-old daughter, Leela. I was sitting on the very same bench where Julia Roberts sat, pregnant, with Hugh Grant at the end of the movie *Notting Hill.* But unlike in the movie, the air wasn't filled with a harmonious serenade of a love song playing as the credits rolled. Amid the birds twittering, nearly everyone within earshot could hear me screaming, "No!" at the top of my lungs.

"Peter!" I shrieked to my husband, who was on the other side of the park. "Follow Leela, *now.* She will fall off the slide! There are no wood chips, just rock-solid dirt. *Now!*" Jumping up from the bench with difficulty, triplet whalesized at twenty-five weeks, I tried to waddle my way over to make sure that he looked after her properly. Somehow, a calm, contented, and pregnant Julia Roberts character holding Hugh Grant's hand didn't mirror my experience of real parenthood.

In the film, on that bench, Julia Roberts observed, "Some people *do* spend their whole lives together." That is what I assumed. I thought that my husband and I would be together forever. But my husband, a fairly well-known movie and TV writer, died when the triplets were one and a half and my older daughter was four. He took the children to the park to play one day; that night he had a stroke, and a day later he was dead.

My world had changed in an instant. I didn't have time to deal with the shock. (I will grieve when I have some spare time—when the kids are all in college.) I was suddenly alone in charge of four very young children. Fortunately, I wasn't the kind of widow who feels very small, drowning in a sea of decisions and worries. I rose to the challenge to become supermom. I would fix every problem and avert every threat to my children. I would protect them. On a nightly basis, I took stock of the upcoming day and assembled "dangers and solutions" to be ready for everything. However, in becoming Supermom, I inadvertently became paranoid mom, the walking encyclopedia of dangers.

Paranoid parents are not wimps; they are warriors without a priority list. I was no cowering wimp. I was smart and committed and a fighter. I was determined to tackle every danger—small and large—with ultimate force.

I moved the children from London to Breckenridge, Colorado. I loved London before I had children, living with its history in the theater and film world. But once I had children, it was a different London with its enormous costs, air pollution, city dangers, terrorism (which killed two people just blocks from our house), high security, high unemployment, low salaries, and an overall lower standard of living. Breckenridge, in contrast, was a beautiful resort town with internationally acclaimed schools, big backyards, bike lanes, sidewalks, and neighborhoods filled with kids—a child-friendly paradise.

I expected a return to peace and quiet but found just the opposite. Most American parents, it seemed, wanted to send their kids to school in bubble wrap. I loved my new friends, but I found many "meerkat moms," constantly on edge from invisible dangers, twitchily watching their children play in the front yard. I saw mothers who panicked if, after doing ballet, soccer, music enrichment, baby French, and yoga, they didn't have time for Your Baby Can Read lessons that day.

You'd think I would have fit right in. But these parents came up with dangers that had never occurred to me. Did I need to buy a walking helmet? Should I have an inch-thick floor pad to prevent skinned knees? Should I remove all the toxic carpet? Is it a good idea to get my kindergartner a cell phone for emergency calls? Are dolls without eyes, noses, and mouths important to allow true imaginative development? It was as though these parents had loaded their brain iPods with every danger that had ever been on the nightly news, *Oprah*, Twitter, or TV dramas.

Knowledge Is Power, but Information Is Not Knowledge

One day I had a revelation as a news story blared on TV; every channel was blasting the headline TEEN GIRL SUICIDE DOUBLES. Immediately my mind went into panic mode. *That has got to be something to worry about! I'd better start thinking about it now, since my girls will be teens in four years and six years, respectively.* But then I stopped to think. *Doubled from what?* Yet the news (or Oprah or Dr. Phil) didn't tell me straight out.

The real statistics were hard to find: doubled from 54 to 106. That was terrible, but "doubled" as the headline said was misleading. One hundred out of 10 million girls is not a lot. For comparison, I researched the statistics for boys that age. It was nearly 3,000 suicides a year! Suicide ranked *third* as the cause of death for teenage boys, but not for teenage girls. So why the exaggerated headline? And, more important for my situation, what were the many more likely dangers to befall my girls? The news made teen girl suicide sound like a probability instead of a remote possibility.

All along, I had been filing away every danger I heard in my brain as equal to every other. I never thought to *prioritize* the dangers. I wanted to fight everything possible. But some of the dangers in my head might not be relevant at all. That was when I decided to question my worries. I read every statistical survey I could find. I consulted with the world's top health and safety experts to find out what was valid information and what was not.

I decided to turn off the worry noise and stop listening to the worry chatter in favor of the facts—from Centers for Disease Control (CDC) statistics, Food and Drug Administration (FDA) reports, World Health Organization (WHO) experts, medical agencies, and hospital reports. What shocked me was that the agencies I went to for confirmation unanimously complained that the studies with clear, helpful information were getting lost or buried by media, manufacturers, and politicians who wanted to go for the sensational.

After years of research, I opened the Paranoid Parent Stop Worrying Shoppe. Our goal was to help parents worry less and prevent the true dangers.

Welcome to Paranoid Parents Anonymous

Picture Meg Ryan's perfect little shop in the movie *You've Got Mail*: warm and fuzzy, cocoa serving, and child nurturing in the golden glow of Pottery Barn antiques. That was my store.

Denver business columnists said that the store was the best model for a business they had ever heard of. We did the research, checked the recalls and consumer studies, and came up with the best product in every category, vetting as well for necessity. (Do you *really* need this safety product or this educational toy?)

We carried things like the only acceptable jogging stroller (and there *is* only one), the safest helmet, formaldehyde-free toys, talking games to keep teens' conversational skills up, the best lead test kit, baby slings for dads, complete Scout camp kits so you didn't have to run to a dozen stores to fill an impossibly long list before a campout, the best mittens and socks to ensure that your child lasted more than ten minutes in the snow, and colorful safety T-shirts so that grandparents could keep track of their grandchildren in a public place.

What began as a storefront became a comedy club and a haven for worried parents. On packed weekends, parents took turns confessing their favorite worry stories to roars of knowing laughter. It became an unofficial Paranoid Parents Anonymous meeting place to discuss real dangers and shed frivolous fears, while children made alphabet letters out of nontoxic gluten-free dough.

People left laughing and usually with some extra souvenirs:

the PARANOID PARENT ON BOARD bumper sticker and a NO WHINING button. Some dads even took extra Paranoid Parents shopping bags to show around at work. Just as in the movie *You've Got Mail*, I had to close the store eventually, but we are still online. We actually outlasted the big anonymous children's superstore in the area, which closed with the recession.

In spite of my evolution from paranoid mom to expert non-worrier, I have managed to raise pretty normal kids. I am bringing up my four children, plus an enormous dog, in a suburban neighborhood in Denver with public schools, no nanny, and each kid trying one (okay, four) activities a term. My kids have surpassed any dream or plans I could have imagined. Each is so much more extraordinary and wonderful than I ever could have anticipated. They are so worth protecting, but they don't deserve a paranoid mother.

I would love to say that this book will stop you from worrying. But let's be realistic: would anything ever completely stop you from worrying about your kids? This is a book about how you can worry less. It is a book about changing *you*, not your child. Many of us buy books about the "gifted child," the "explosive child," the "defiant child," or about children who can't sleep, can't read, aren't potty trained, and so on. These books tell you how to change your child, but few books explore how *you* are coping. This book fills that gap.

The cover may say that it is about raising resilient children, and I hope that this will happen. But first we need to become resilient parents. This book is about changing how you feel without pills, relaxation sessions, a glass of wine, and any other short-term worry fixes.

Real and perceived dangers will happen. The unexpected presents itself daily. How you experience those scares, threats, and false alarms makes the difference between a happy parent and a totally overwhelmed or overworried one.

Paranoia describes an exaggerated, irrational, and persistent fear. We will fix this type of fear not with deep breathing or frantic childproofing, but with the facts. The goal of this book is to put your worries into proper perspective and help you worry less. When you are able to give yourself a thorough reality check, your common sense can get back in line with the real world.

Chapter Two

Worry Crazy Makers

"Be careful whom you trust." There spoke a true paranoid. I am not a conspiracy theorist, but I am suggesting that not all of the information in this information age is so reliable.

I'm not accusing the rich and powerful of trying to brainwash us. That really sounds paranoid. It isn't a conspiracy. "It's only business." Fear sells big. As in the movie *Monsters, Inc*, scaring is big business. Scaring people makes them vote a certain way, persuades them to buy things, and keeps them glued to the media. The media, the companies, and the politicians have jobs to do. Doing their jobs means persuading people to watch, to buy, and to vote. The more vividly they paint dangers, the more persuasive and successful they are at their jobs.

What's more significant is that the media, the manufacturers, and the politicians don't sell the cure; they sell the prevention. Then they can claim that they saved you when nothing happens—when there are no national sniper outbreaks, no pandemics, no kitchen fires (because you had stove knob protectors), and no shower falls (because you had toddler shower boots). They convince you that they have saved you from something that was actually *never going to happen in the first place*.

Happiness is a motivator, but it's not as powerful as fear. "I will make you happy if you watch, buy, or vote" doesn't have the same impact as "This terrible thing happened once; it will happen again, and it could wipe out your world as you know it—if you don't watch, buy, or vote." They aren't lying; they just aren't putting the fears into perspective.

The Media: Replaying the Worst-Case Scenario of Your Worst Nightmares

The guiding ethos of journalism is "If it bleeds, it leads."

Sensational Stories Yield the Highest Ratings

Sensational stories are usually the rarest threats, but they are replayed so often that they seem to happen daily. For instance, the tragic story of Madeleine McCann, a British girl who was kidnapped from her hotel room in Portugal in 2007, made it seem as though kidnappings are the norm, because daily news reports about it went on for months or even years. When a school sniper story replays for months every night, it seems that school shootings are a daily event, when in reality they are exceptionally rare occurrences.

A New Global Threat Every Day

Do you remember the scares that were going to wipe out humanity? What was the devastation done by each disease? Mad cow disease: 3 U.S. cases but no deaths, and 200 deaths worldwide; SARS: no U.S. deaths, 74 deaths worldwide. These were all top news stories of pandemics that were supposedly set to wipe out humanity and thus had us panicked. Pandemics and the possibility of total annihilation keeps you glued to the TV set. It also distracts you from real dangers.

Warning Labels on News Stories?

Imagine that you are watching a news story about West Nile disease. A warning like the following should come up at the bottom of the screen: WEST NILE FLU—AGES 1–15, NO REPORTED CASES. Then, at the end of every story, instead of a media-celebrity expert blowing up the dangers so you buy his or her book, the go-to person should be a risk analyst who explains how likely it is that the danger du jour will actually happen.

Thank goodness that anthrax never became a widespread national killer—or SARS, or mad cow disease, or any of the pandemics or disaster scenarios, from weather to terrorism. Yet the news never reports when these projected threats fail to materialize. No retractions are ever published. It might be embarrassing to make a retraction after the massive coverage that was given to the warning of each week's impending-doom, worst-case scenario.

Alerts to Dangers, Not Relevance

The danger of children suffering brain damage from sucking repeatedly on plastic shower curtains led our local news channel to launch a campaign against "The Great Indoors." Bad plastic, kids suck on things: it has to be a problem. But children would have to suck on the bad plastic for *three to four hours* to get to the level deemed worrisome by the FDA. The odds of a child sucking on a shower curtain for four hours are pretty low (I would hope). But instead of taking on the plastics industry, or easier still, suggesting that parents *watch their kids*, the news channel sounded noble for launching a campaign against the evil purveyors of toxic shower curtains, complete with a blog, a petition, and proposed meetings with company officials.

After hearing the news story, for a split second, I almost ran upstairs to check my shower curtains. But instead, I put the worry into perspective. The issue might be something that I want to be aware of, but it was not an imminent evil to fight. Unfortunately, parents are often sent on ridiculous campaigns to fight the evil nothing.

Remember this when you hear a horrific news story: a sensational tragedy that plays endlessly on the news has happened *once*. It is not taking place in every neighborhood every day. Because it has happened once doesn't mean that it will repeat everywhere every day. The news story is repeated endlessly; the crime does not repeat endlessly, everywhere. Most of these events are evil nothings that should not be on parents' danger radar.

Commerce: Can There Be Too Much Worry in This Fearful Time?

There's no such thing as too much worry, according to the Intelligence Group, a market research and trend consulting firm that advises companies on the psychology of selling to today's parents. Fear is how you sell to parents. The message of the Intelligence Group for manufacturers is to tell parents that we are "parenting during a particularly fearful time." I find it shocking that companies put together scare campaigns. Maybe I am naive.

The group's Mom Intelligence Survey tells us that we are really "completely helpless against the dangers threatening our children." Worry is all around us.

A simple trip to the airport surrounds us with a cocoon of fear: code-orange alerts, full-body searches, X-ray machines. Ads warn us that our children won't be smart enough, that our homes require baby proofing, that certain products will kill all germs, that our toddler needs a helmet to learn how to walk. Worry, buy. Even many parenting magazines are full of fearful reading material, with every story exposing a danger and every ad promising to alleviate a danger, from the wrong baby formula to diaper rash cream to a college savings plan for your newborn. Worry, read.

Is this an exceptionally fearful time? Are we really under direct threats every

Tension Tamer:

Every nightly news story is not a reason to panic. Consider the relevance in your own life and choose your worries wisely. Don't waste your worry on the evil nothing.

WORRY LESS TIP:

Look for motives behind the dire warnings. Be careful whom you trust. Remember that most of these companies could sell air conditioners to Eskimos.

moment? In my focus groups with worried parents, I've heard from parents who have stayed awake all night worrying about visiting a theme park (kidnappers, murderers, dangerous rides) and parents who drove the middle school principal crazy demanding that their child be placed in the safest seat in each class in case a sniper came into the school. I've met parents who had their homes environmentally cleaned for $50,000 a year, parents who moved away from the New York City area the year after 9/11, and Los Angeles parents who won't go to the beach for fear of a shark attack. These are fearful behaviors.

Surveys and focus groups, spending reports, and trends confirm that we have bought the fear and helplessness message—hook, line, and sinker. We feel under siege as parents and act as though we are in attacking-lion or -lioness mode to protect our kids every minute of every day.

Politicians

Politicians, ideally, want to improve the country, so they naturally point out what is wrong in order to get you to vote for them. That makes sense, but it can have a detrimental effect. The more vivid the portrayal of a problem or a danger, the more likely you are to vote for whoever you think can fix the problem. If the problem is portrayed at its worst, you will be running to the polls.

Exaggerating problems is not ethical, but it happens with the best intentions. I won't go into the evildoings of political parties to illustrate. Many award-winning books, such as *False Alarm: The Truth About the Epidemic of Fear* by Dr. Marc Siegel or *The Culture of Fear: Why Americans Are Afraid of the Wrong Things* by Barry Glassner, focus on these issues. The fact that political parties scare us into voting is a problem. They exploit our feelings on a particularly emotive worry and pledge to solve it to earn our votes, which further distorts our view of reality and real dangers. Nevertheless, I am going to throw some of the blame back on us. The consequence of believing sensational stories on the news and hearsay scare stories is that we want politicians to solve what we perceive to be wrong rather than the real dangers our society faces.

In this way, we are like small children who are afraid of the monsters under the bed. The parents know that there are no monsters under the bed, but they will give the child a cuddle, a glass of milk, or a new stuffed toy. Sometimes they will even lie down and sleep with the child to quiet him or her.

We are similarly obsessive and panicked about potential pandemics, killer kids, killer tomatoes, toxic lettuce, crime, terrorists, and school snipers—all dangers grossly out of proportion—and politicians have to appear to solve these nonproblems to get our votes and make us happy. Spending lots of time, energy, and funds to give the appearance of fixing these negligible dangers leaves less time, energy, and funds for tackling truly crucial matters.

The real-world effect of this thinking is that we put money into obscure causes. The "Here's a problem—quick, do something, anything" approach leads to misapplied funds and unintended consequences that can be worse than the original problem or even worse than doing nothing.

Danger Sociology 101: Informational Cascade Theory

Informational cascade theory explains why we, a group of rational people, can get something totally wrong—whether it's the housing bubble or the autism or vaccine question. It explains why we can act like lemmings following the herd, the celebrity, or the politician.

Following the leader used to be the right, smart thing to do. We have put our faith in the chieftain since caveman days. But it can go very wrong when the information is partial or the leaders have their own agendas. So we believe the guru, the politician, or the celebrity who may have a particular cause, which isn't the most important cause, or the news anchor who reports the sensational story. One individual follows, and more and more join. It is, at heart, rational to follow, but the result is a massive social copying that can go completely wrong. We turn into lemmings plunging off the cliff for all the seemingly right reasons.

Everyone can't be wrong, we think. Yes, they can—with the best intentions, perhaps, but they are still totally incorrect.

In science and sociology this is called *informational cascade*. We think of it as a fad or a trend, but it results in a massive epidemic of misinformation. The group mind quickly turns into a mob, with heightened physical behavior that often has tragic results.

Many of these cascades are proving potentially devastating for society. People who follow the advice of certain celebrities who suggest that we shouldn't get our children vaccinated will cause a health crisis. We must act together as a herd to make the right choices and not go back to a time of polio, measles, and mumps. These are not personal decisions.

> WORKY LESS TIP:
> Trust your common sense! It's the most inexpensive child protection on the market.

The use of car seats and the prevention of drunk driving are societal issues.

We need to look at dangers in a local or a national context. Everything is presented as a danger with no context.

As a herd, we need to look at the cold, hard facts; only then can we champion the right causes. We might need a college degree in sociology and statistics to understand the equations that explain why we follow false beliefs, but we have hugely misdirected funds and efforts by jumping on the wrong bandwagon.

Ourselves: Stop Scaring One Another Senseless

In my visits with parents across the country, I have found that the oath of moms at morning coffee-shop sessions seems to be this: "I believe that there is a stranger or a danger lurking around every corner." Mothers need coffee meetings for sanity, not for scaring one another senseless with statements like the following:

• "H1N1 vaccine for kids is past its sell-by date and ineffective!"
• "Sixteen kids a day get shot at school."
• "Window blinds have all been recalled."
• "The principal is holding a meeting about pedophiles moving into the area."

We often believe that there really is a danger or a stranger lurking around every corner to come after our children. Pedophiles hiding in department store clothes racks ready to jump out and expose themselves to your child, lone children on theme park rides being snatched in the dark, vaccinations that must be harmful because a much-loved personality said so, or the expulsion of twenty middle school girls for performing oral sex on boys at recess—all these tales, and more, are discussed at morning coffee sessions. The parents leave shocked and shattered.

Many parents are in defense mode when they go to the grocery store or walk around the neighborhood for trick-or-treating. Our adrenaline is rushing, our nerves are on edge, and we are barking "Stay close, walk in front of me, six-foot limit" military campaign orders to our kids when we walk downtown. We are at war against the criminal.

Phew, I made it home from the mall without a kidnapping or an assault, you think, relieved. But even when you've arrived home, you tell your kids, "No, you can't scooter in the driveway. Someone [bad] might be out there."

Worshipping the Worry God

A grandmother told me that she never shopped with her three-year-old grandson. They simply mall walked. I thought, *How fantastic*—the exercise, going to shops without actually buying. But, she continued proudly, as if to show that she was the best grandma in the world, "I would never shop, because I would have to let go of his hand while I talked and paid the clerk. He could get kidnapped while my head was turned."

I pointed out the low odds of this happening, but her response was, "If I didn't worry constantly, and something happened, I would blame myself forever. I have to think about it every minute." She couldn't just happily hold his hand, if she thought she should, and enjoy her time with her grandson; she had to be anxious and ever vigilant. Xena Warrior Grandma. Somehow, the more she worried, the better a grandparent she was. Why do we feel that worrying appeases some worry god?

The Five Ugly Truths About Worrying

1. Your worries are not safety shields. If you worry "enough," your child will *not* be protected by an invisible force field.

2. Worry does not appease the worry god.

3. Worry in itself is passive and does nothing to solve the problem.

4. Worrying more doesn't mean that you love your child more.

5. Worrying often expresses itself as nagging, which sours your relationship with your child.

We cling to our worries like safety shields. If we worry enough, we think our children will be miraculously protected by an invisible force field. Yet even though worry-penance time may get you into worry heaven when you are dead, it won't stop injuries and accidents. When it comes to safety, you largely make your own luck for yourself and your child.

Worrying is an addiction to some, almost a religion to others. We each believe that our child could be the one to be the victim of a school sniper more than we believe that the sun rises in the east. *I dare not disturb that worldview, because something bad will befall me for doubting it,* thinks the superstitious parent.

This chapter has explored how our society has worked us up into this state. The next chapter will show you why this is harmful to you and your kids.

Chapter Three

Why Worry Is Dangerous: The Science of the Fear Epidemic

There are more than 35 million families with children in the United States. When divorced, separated, and non-married parents are added in, parents total over 92 million. They are looking after 74 million children under eighteen or 83 million children if you count eighteen-year-olds. In addition to parents and guardians who worry about their kids, there are about 56 million grandparents, most of whom are actively involved with their grandchildren. That adds up to about 150 million people who are directly concerned with or worrying about the nation's children. That is half of the population.

If each person could list twenty worries per child, that would add up to 3 billion worries going unchecked and largely undirected. If we have 3 billion unchecked worries, this means that a lot of people are needlessly stressed out, striving for solutions for a multitude of "dangers."

Paranoia: How a Cycle of Worry Becomes an Addiction

Having a newborn and a toddler to worry about doesn't give a mom or a dad much time to keep up with anything else. The sleepless nights of worry and constant phobias, largely perceived and not real, are, according to many experts, characteristic of American parents today. We are so busy worrying that we don't notice that everyone else is worrying. Nobel prize winners have researched American's devotion to worry. Many "fear" book titles are published. The rest of the world is baffled by Americans' obsessive worrying. We need to question if what we are worrying about is valid. It is not just about our children but about every-thing that we perceive as dangerous.

Worry Happens to Incredibly Intelligent People

An expert knows a lot about one thing. But parents need to be experts in everything: swine flu, nutrition, first aid, conflict reso-lution, sports coaching, reading and math instruction, bicycle assembly, and how to get to level seven on the Nintendo DS *Indiana Jones* game.

I'll bet you have a solution for every danger, in spite of your self-doubts. Even before your children were born, you probably were on the Internet, diligently researching plastics, food prepa-ration, and cloth diapers, and had registered for at least 200 baby "essentials." If you didn't do these things, you're certainly feeling the need to make up for lost time now that your kids are pre-kindergarten age. Oh, the guilt from not buying the GPS child-tracking device (this alerts you if your child is out of range). Stop yourself! Your child doesn't need a ten-pound fake watch, and you don't need to track him or her within six inches of his or her location. Really. *Really*.

Parents are so hard on themselves. They are kid and product experts, but they still label themselves with politically incorrect epithets like *helicopter parents, alpha moms, "competi" dads, slacker dads* and *slacker moms, smother mothers,* and *soccer moms*. You would never speak so rudely to a stranger, but you are incredibly hard on yourself.

This self-doubt, this guilt about never doing enough and never being the best, drives you to want to know everything. When you're at home with a helpless baby, knowing it all makes you feel in control and intellectually satisfied—even if it is based on a fear that you're not protecting your most valuable "possession"—and the result is a constant hyper state.

Worry Happens When There Is a Lot to Lose

Everything does seem important when we value our children as priceless. We are lavish in our protectiveness, showing pride and glee about these children we obsess about. Each of us thinks that our child is so special that he or she will be the one child that every kidnapper will take. We think that our child is the most blessed yet the most vulnerable to dangers. And, heaven forbid, our child doesn't stand out as being as special to others as he or she is to us.

We have much in common with animals when it comes to our instinctive response to threats—this is known as the fight-or-flight instinct. We perceive a possible threat, and we immediately go into the "danger countdown," with different areas of the brain triggering as the possible threat is confirmed. But our brains do differ from the brains of animals, thanks to our great intellect. Not only will we respond if we see a bear or an oncoming car, we can hear a warning from a friend, see a photo of a teen selling drugs to kids, read a newspaper article on guns, or see a movie on child pornography, and our mind reads those as being immediate threats to survival. Our mind accepts them as threats that are just as real as a tiger jumping over the zoo fence and coming after our kids or a rattlesnake slithering toward us on a hiking trip.

So you see a TV show about a danger, and your body kicks into that fight-or-flight survival protocol. Your metabolism changes, different areas of the brain click on like some automatic preflight sequence for a space shuttle. You think that your survival is threatened. The middle brain doesn't distinguish a big threat from a little threat. It just sends you running or fighting. When you are controlled by the middle brain, you are freaked out by anything.

And that is bad. We live in a perpetual state of low-level stress that can easily be triggered by the smallest worry and escalate into full-blown anxiety.

Some parent worry may come from being a new parent. With "no prior experience" on your new-parent résumé, you will be more stressed and more worried, and the worry cycle will take hold. It's also never ending: you will have the same "no prior experience" anxiety for each new phase that your first child enters—toddler years, elementary school years, the "tweens," the teens, and even the college years.

Sensationalism, marketing, inexperience, and irrational love all contribute to the underlying problem we have with our flight-or-flight instinctive survival skills meeting up with our overstimulated, thinking brains. Only lots of practice prioritizing worries and calming down will set up a new pattern in our survival matrix.

Worrying a Little Makes You Worry More

When people feel threatened, the brain lights up like Las Vegas. Worry manifests in psychological and physiological reactions that are concrete—not figments of an overtired parent's imagination. The heart beats faster. When we get really scared, the middle brain, as noted earlier, lights up, and the rational brain clicks off like a total power failure.

When you feel threatened but are not able to act on it and resolve it (for instance, because it is a TV killer, not a real one), the chemicals in the body build up. You start living with low-level stress; then small threats boost the stress levels to higher levels than normal, and the stress builds faster and leaves stronger anxiety.

Low-level stress thus instigates a cycle. Once we worry about one thing, it becomes easy to have a second worry and then a third, sending our bodies and our brains into a cycle of worry—even if the concerns aren't valid. We worry more and more, and worry feeds worry.

Worry addiction isn't like other addictions in which you need a bigger and bigger "fix" because your body builds up immunity. Worry is just the opposite. Your system doesn't build up a tolerance to worry and stress, because they are part of your survival instincts. Once you are in a worry cycle, instead of taking more and more worry to get you to a frantic state, it takes less and less—and the franticness of the state increases. If you are in a very anxious state, a news story on TV can make you hysterical even when absolutely nothing has happened.

With every potential threat, the middle brain lights up like a pinball machine. You have learned to worry more. This is why a parent who is hyped with worry cannot react properly in a real emergency. Being a paranoid fixer of every danger, rather than just the rational few, is dangerous in itself; then there is also what it does to your children.

Family Impact: Why Is Little Janey Wearing Bubble Wrap to Kindergarten?

Before you had children, did you list as one of your life goals "to be the most worried parent in the United States"? Parents boast that they love their children so much that they don't sleep at night because they're worrying. Parents confuse worrying with actually taking productive steps. They equate worry with love. Parents believe that worrying is doing something, yet it's often the opposite. Even worse, worrying creates over-the-top parents:

1. We *over*protect so our little dear is safe and happy.
2. We *over*program so our little one is an expert in sports, languages, music, and art.
3. We *over*control so our little precious doesn't make a wrong (unsafe) decision.
4. We *over*spend so we have every tool to ensure the safest, smartest, most popular child. We will go into debt to buy the safest and best of everything.

These best intentions are really worry driven; they come from fears and insecurities that our children won't be safe and successful.

If your body chemistry survival mechanism has gone awry and you are turning into a worry addict, it can affect your child. However much parents try to conceal their worries—and most don't, most deliberately advertise their worry—each cue that a parent is tensing, avoiding, warning, and gasping acts like a little worry shock to the child. Even if the child is not actively involved in the worry, he or she cannot escape it and will internalize it. A raised voice can cue a child into fear, and soon the child will have a compounding anxiety cycle. He or she has anxiety with no healthy outlets and may become trapped in a worsening kid-level worry cycle.

Have You Become Over-the-Top?

Are you guilty of any of the following over-the-top parenting traits? If so, how many of them might be driven by fear and worry? How can you let some of them go?

1. You have never been on a vacation on your own, without the kids.

2. You have never hired a babysitter outside family members.

3. You have made your child's home world resemble a theme park (Wiis, Playstations, a karaoke machine, a princess boutique bedroom that even *Extreme Makeover* host Ty Pennington could not have accomplished).

4. You spent more energy planning your child's birthday party than your wedding, with the best cupcakes, gift bags, and live ponies for the bash.

5. You scrimped and saved to get two-year-old Ella to Disneyland.

6. You've turned your life over to be a kid chauffeur.

7. You stayed up until 2:00 AM to research the best baby swaddling sacks.

It starts, for example, with the parents saying to their child, "Watch the coffee table corner. We don't use markers. Don't run—it's slippery. That is glass. Is that the right plastic?" It ends with the parents flying out to talk to the child's college freshman chemistry teacher about the C their child received on his or her first assignment. Colleges report an epidemic of parents flying out "to the rescue" for the most trivial matters. We are creating a generation of children who are old enough to get a learner's permit for driving but have never crossed a street by themselves.

Reality Check
✓Even low-level constant stress doesn't make for a happy parent, nor does it make a resilient, resourceful child who believes that he or she can control his world.

Teaching Helplessness

Imagine that every time you express a fear of something to your child or warn about some danger, you are giving him or her an electric shock that will eventually create a helpless child. That's the modern theory of learned helplessness in its most popularized form.

The theory is very, very complex and is just in the early stages of development. Psychologists use it accurately, but many in the mainstream press—me included—use it haphazardly. Nevertheless, it is still an effective concept even if one doesn't understand the nuances of the theory.

The basic theory—this is guaranteed to make you cringe—
comes from giving random electric shocks to dogs. The dogs
learned to behave against what we would consider the nature of
the dog (as well as humans) to fight or flee. Because there was
great hurt but no pattern, these dogs sensed that they could do
nothing to stop the pain and became passive, helpless, and hope-
less. They didn't try to escape the shocks but would simply lie
there and be shocked.

People have similar reactions to random events. Most people
try to impose some order on totally random events. Other
people acknowledge that the events are random and not the
result of fate, sent by God, self-created, or deserved because of
some bad personal action. These people maintain a sense of control over their lives and deal with random misfortune as it comes.

Some people become passive when they are presented with
real negative, random events or with imagined events over which
they feel no control. Children too can become passive if they
don't learn a sense of control in the world.

Teaching Billy That He Can't ...

If you teach Billy that he can't climb a tree, you can mistakenly take it too far and teach Billy that he can't control his world.
There are three ways we teach helplessness.

The first way is to take control away from our children by
making them believe that the world is too tough or that they

need constant assistance. The following statements are ways in which we might do this:

- "I'll do that for you."
- "I'll put the batteries in for you."
- "I put a snack in your backpack."
- "I'll get your socks and gloves so you won't freeze."
- "I will talk to the teacher if you want."

The second way we teach helplessness is to present the world as frightening. This can teach our children passivity, an inability to cope, and the concept that the world is beyond their control. Here are some examples of the constant nagging that comes from our mouths:

- "Don't go too close to the lake, you could fall in."
- "Don't play in the front yard, there may be strangers."
- "Watch out for the big kids, they play rough."
- "Turn off the lights, they could cause a fire."
- "You're going to get hit in the head by a ball."

Third, we allow them to overhear comments from those around them and then don't offer explanations, which can frighten children into believing the world is too dangerous. This might include the following:

- Parents talking in hushed voices about predators
- Sniper proofing at school
- Hearing "Terror level: orange" at the airport

- Airport body searches
- Parents talking about frightening news stories

Learned helplessness is a vivid term for us to keep in mind to moderate our paranoid inclinations to protect our children, warn our children, and do everything for our children that they should be learning to master themselves. It's important to ask yourself, *Am I teaching them that they are helpless in the face of the new and unknown?*

Low self-esteem and depression are two common outcomes that appear in college, especially, if not throughout the child's entire academic career. If Mom and Dad get the mail, go along on field trips, nag the child not to talk to strangers, or recount their fears of flying, each of these is a random shock to the child, reinforcing the notion that it is a big, bad world out there. It's just like the shocks that were given to the dogs in the study. Each worry shock removes the child's control of his or her world and deprives the child of the challenges that an individual needs to learn to overcome to take on life's responsibilities.

> **WORRY LESS TIP:**
> Before you speak to your children, try to self-censor all the paranoid safety instructions.

Whether it's "afraid of the world" paranoid fears, a "you need mom" forced clinging mode, or a well-meaning "I will take care of you in this big world," all teach helplessness.

Raising a Mouse or a Hell's Angel

The flip side of creating a helpless young adult is creating a thrill seeker. Numbed for years by an endless monologue of "Don't do that—it's dangerous!" about absolutely everything, your child now believes that nothing is dangerous because he or she never got hurt from all those things you went on about.

For example, my PARANOID PARENT ON BOARD bumper sticker is my attempt to poke a little fun at the BABY ON BOARD bumper sticker—the bumper sticker of the true paranoid parents, who are announcing to the world, "Watch out for my car, because my precious baby is in it." It explains their overcautious, neurotic driving. People come up to me in parking lots, at gas pumps, and everywhere to talk about the PARANOID PARENT ON BOARD bumper sticker.

I was driving with my kids on a country road when we were suddenly surrounded by a biker gang of twentysomethings. There were about two dozen of them, gunning their engines. It was truly a paranoid parent's nightmare. We had to stop at a stop sign, and they drove around us whooping and agitated. By this time my kids were really scared. I was, too.

One biker came up to my window. "That is the greatest bumper sticker we have ever seen," he said. "Our parents were all paranoid parents. It drove us crazy. Look at us now. Great bumper

Tension Tamer:

Your job as a parent is not to keep your child safe and happy all the time. Your job is to prepare your child to do things without you. Your child needs to take risks.

> **WORRY LESS TIP:**
>
> Have lots of hugs and bandages ready. Engage in some controlled risk taking: Walk behind your child as he or she tries to find the way home, or oversee making breakfast until your child has mastered the tasks. Your son or daughter's self-esteem will improve if you don't interfere.

sticker, lady!" They all cheered and nodded, then waved good-bye and roared off, leaving us sitting there speechless.

In order to help you break the worry cycle, the next chapter will give you a reality check to see if your top worries are even worth worrying about. Who knows, you might enjoy parenting more—and even get some sleep.

Chapter Four

Myths Exposed: Parents' Top Worries Versus Children's Real Dangers

A woman over forty is more likely to be killed by a terrorist than get married. Well, it sounds true.

Many of us remember Meg Ryan's worries in the movie *Sleepless in Seattle* (no doubt, I do watch too many Meg Ryan movies). What sounds like it should be true often is not. However, do not feel stupid, misinformed, or ignorant. Remember that the perceived dangers are what most people believe.

Too many Americans conclude from all the misinformation and uncertainty that the world is a hostile place. It is an uncertain, unpredictable place, but that is not the same as a hostile world from which we must shield ourselves and our loved ones.

Absolutely Crazy Notions

Take a quiz. How many of the following make the list of your top ten concerns for your children?

1. Kidnapping
2. School snipers
3. Terrorism
4. Stranger danger
5. Drugs
6. Vaccinations
7. Playing in the front yard or walking to school
8. Bullying
9. School buses
10. Natural disasters

Is this really the top-ten list of dangers? Do you agree with many of these? If so, you would be wrong but not alone. This was the list of the perceived top ten dangers based on our focus group and survey lists of parents' worries. This closely matches many national and international polls, including a British-commissioned Ipos MORI (Market & Opinion Research International) poll, and a *Time* magazine article.

In addition, Paranoid Parents polled local news stations in the Denver area, researching what the main dangers to children must be, based on the stories that are covered most prevalently. They are as follows:

1. Kidnapping
2. Child snipers, school shootings, or terrorism
3. Murder
4. Stranger danger

5. Drugs, sex, and alcohol

6. Drowning

7. Teenage driver incidents

8. Gangs

Now here is the reality checklist—the real causes of death and injury for most children:

1. Car accidents

2. Homicide (but not from snipers or kidnappers; young inner-city men are the usual victims)

3. Maltreatment or abuse (usually by a family member, not a stranger)

4. Suicide

5. Drowning

6. Fire

7. Suffocation

8. Bicycle accidents

9. Unintentional poisoning

10. Everything else

This makes it clear that many parents are wasting their time worrying about the wrong things. Are you?

National and international surveys show that parents, me included, have not the vaguest grasp on the real-world dangers that threaten their children. The top twenty things that parents worry about bear no relation to what is most likely to endanger their children.

Here is firm ground for you to stand on. Get your danger list aligned with reality. We all need a worry-perception tune-up to fix the indiscriminate approach to dangers that we have developed.

Let us start the reality check. Each parent-perceived worry is followed by the corresponding real danger in rank.

Parents' Worry Number 1: Kidnapping

For parents, there is no bigger dread than the kidnapping of their child. This is a topic we are so superstitious about that we hardly dare speak of it. We are most afraid of strangers who kidnap, rape, and murder children under ten. Propelling our instincts in this area are the dreadful worst-case-scenario stories that fill the media—coverage that often drives ratings but doesn't accurately reflect the statistics of kidnapping.

The Mayo Clinic of Rochester, Minnesota, reported that three-fourths of the parents who were surveyed feared that their children would be abducted, and one-third said that this was a frequent fear. In parent surveys, the fear of kidnapping ranks greater than the fears of car accidents, sports injuries, or drug addiction—dangers that are *far more likely* to happen.

This fear isn't surprising when we hear that over 850,000 children in the United States disappear each year. The website missingchild.wordpress.com claims that number is 1.3 million or almost one in fifty children. Law enforcement gives the median "average" as 2,100 children a day. No wonder we are fingerprinting our children and holding on to them for dear life when we go to the mall, on vacation, or even just out the front door.

It's important to know that *missing* doesn't mean *kidnapped*. Parent-scaring media and protection companies have the "real" kidnapping number readily at hand: about 262,000 children a year. One in 285 children will be kidnapped? That too is terrifying, but is it correct?

Reality Check

✓ It's important for parents to know the true data on child kidnappings so that they can protect their children from real threats and also worry less. Our perception is that many young children are actually being kidnapped and murdered daily, but they are not.

So who is taking children? The following statistics are from the National Center for Missing and Exploited Children 2002:

- Missing, under age eighteen: 855,700
- Kidnapping by family member: 203,900
- Kidnapping by non–family member: 58,200
- Stereotypical kidnapping (i.e., by a stranger who transports the child over 50 miles and holds overnight): 110 (or 115 to allow for a margin of error, of which approximately 40 percent are killed)
- Age breakdown of stereotypical kidnappings:

  | 1–5 years old: 20 | 12–14 years old: 45 |
  | 6–11 years old: 25 | 15–17 years old: 20 |

Any kidnapping is one too many, but for that terror to be ever-present in a parent's mind isn't rational, especially when the parent conveys the fear to the child on routine trips to the store or what should be fun family vacations.

The overwhelming number of child kidnappings is perpetrated by family members who take the child from the parent with legal custody. According to the National Center for Missing and Exploited Children, 98 percent of these children are returned.

Non–family member abductions include scenarios like an ex-boyfriend forcing a girl into a car or a babysitter refusing to turn over the three children she is babysitting until she is paid in full. Real kidnappings are rare, and teenage girls are the usual victims.

The AMBER Alert

It isn't just the media and companies that create and profit from erroneous beliefs about child kidnappings. There is also a tool that is meant to assist parents but that actually confuses them about the circumstances of kidnappings. I'm talking about the AMBER Alert.

The AMBER Alert works with federal and law enforcement agencies as well as the media to release bulletins in high-risk child-abduction cases. According to the U.S. Justice Department's website, "The goal of an AMBER Alert is to instantly galvanize the entire community to assist in the search for and the safe recovery of the child."

The AMBER Alert wants parents to sign up for a text message of an alert. This official message supports the idea of a society that is just short of the sci-fi classic *Fahrenheit 451* in which everyone goes out and stands in his or her front yard to catch the criminal.

The AMBER Alert registry advertising is so frightening that you will not only sign up, you will also photograph your child each day as he or she goes to school so that you will be sure to have an up-to-date photo for the police in case anything happens.

"Nothing in this van tells you there is an abducted child inside," the AMBER Alert advertisement reads.

"There is one [kidnapper-murderer] in every area, and they [sic] are just waiting to abduct a child," warned Sheriff Jeff Dawsy of Citrus County, Florida, at the National AMBER Alert Symposium in 2009 in Tampa, Florida.

His reasoning was that if there has been one in one neighborhood, there must be one in every neighborhood.

I'm in favor of *anything* that helps parents to protect their children from harm—one child kidnapped is one too many. The AMBER Alert program *saves children's lives* and makes children's safety a community cause, and there is a critical reason for the rapidly deployed alerts: children are most often murdered within the first three hours of their abduction.

Nevertheless, AMBER Alerts also create an atmosphere that makes parents believe that the kidnapping of children by strangers and the resulting violence is pervasive. It's not. When most people think of AMBER Alerts, they envision a child under ten being kidnapped, abused, and killed by a stranger, but as we saw in the reality check previously, that isn't usually the case.

In 2008, the AMBER Alert had approximately nine cases of stereotypical kidnappings of children under thirteen years old that ended in murder; however, in some of these cases, the parents were implicated but had not been convicted.

What we need is calm education for our children and parents—not paranoid parents and teachers who frighten children with misinformation. What are the best ways to guard your children from stranger abduction?

We are misdirecting our efforts by educating small children because the victims are primarily tween and teenage girls. Even these tragic cases are still extremely remote compared to the other dangers that threaten girls at these ages.

Support the AMBER Alert and respect those who have lost children, but do so with the full knowledge that stereotypical kidnapping is a rare event. In its history, the AMBER Alert has saved 502 children. (Most of these were family kidnappings.) In the last ten years, stereotypical kidnappings have dropped from 300 cases a year to about 100. The worry of getting caught could be a deterrent.

Mostly we need to get it firmly into our heads that kidnapping is not the big fight to fight. It is not the biggest threat to our children. Walking in a store, through a theme park, or at a children's play area, you worry about kidnapping threats. But the actual statistics do not justify our being in a perpetual state of anxiety when we leave the house or tuck in our children at night.

I'm glad that AMBER Alerts have successfully returned some

at-risk children to their parents, but what's interesting to me is that in almost every situation, including kidnappings, simple, pragmatic tools can help the most. Kidnappings are always the transgression of the perpetrator; they are *never* a parent's fault. Yet we can take some simple steps to alleviate our worrying so that we can simply enjoy our kids.

Preventative Tips

Predators often presume that a carefully dressed child is more likely to be consistently watched, and they conclude that taking that child entails a higher risk of arrest, an outcome they don't want. A kidnapper is therefore more likely to abscond with a scruffy child who appears neglected. A scruffy child who is carried away screaming will be mistaken for a bad kid who is misbehaving.

In half of the cases, the kidnappers work as a team in which one person chats with the child to see if the team is likely to lure the child easily.

Teach your children to always say no when they are approached by an adult who asks them to go places or tries to get them into or near a car.

Children must know never to go anywhere with anyone who is not a parent or a teacher without their parents saying it is okay, whether or not they know the person. Children should be taught to immediately tell their parents or a nearby adult if someone is asking them to go somewhere.

Ultimately, if you are panicked about stranger kidnappings

and murders, then you should also be more panicked about your child being struck by lightning, having a heart attack, flipping over in a shopping cart, eating toothpaste, and hundreds of more likely misfortunes that could befall him or her. Between 5,000 and 10,000 children have strokes each year. Do you worry about that daily?

Real Danger Number 1: Car Accidents

The nightly news reports car accidents—the more tragically spectacular, the better. The high incidence of car accidents would be worth worrying about. But this paranoid parents guide is not about worrying, it's about fixing. And the good news is that almost all car accident deaths are the fault of human error and are therefore preventable, to a large extent.

Although the recent incessant news stories have been about faulty cars and car company cover-ups, it isn't faulty cars but people who cause most of the accidents. Often, these people are the parents themselves.

Buckling seat belts is not glamorous. I have four children, and every time we leave the house, no matter how many are in the SUV, no matter what the length of the ride, I make sure that each child is buckled up.

That means climbing through three rows of seats to attend to Leela, who at eight could usually buckle herself, then to Nathan, Zachary, and Abby, my triplets, then six. If you assume that it took a minute and a half to buckle each of my children properly, that's six minutes a car trip, twelve minutes round-trip; if we went to the market and back and made three stops along the way, that's a fair amount of my adult day buckling my childrens' seat belts. It could add nearly an hour to a multistop shopping trip. (Watching them try to buckle themselves, in the freezing cold, and then having to step in to help—well, you can see why it was hard for me not to start the shopping trip as a frustrated wreck.)

Why don't I just slack off? Motor vehicle injuries are the leading cause of death among children under the age of fourteen in the United States, according to the CDC. One of the most tragic aspects of these deaths is that more than 50 percent of the children were not wearing their seat belts. The National Highway Traffic Safety Administration (NHTSA) says that more than half of serious injuries to children, as well as deaths, could be reduced if the children were correctly strapped into the kind of seat that is appropriate for their size.

WORRY LESS TIP:
Buckle your kids in at all times. Buckling is a nonnegotiable must-do, whether you are out of town, in town, or driving to the mailbox. It's necessary all the time, for all ages.

Reality Check

✓ In most fatal car crashes, the children were not buckled in or weren't buckled properly.

Some Statistics

An unbelievable 10 percent of parents think they never have to buckle up their children. For local driving, it's estimated that more than half of parents think that buckling up is too much trouble. But "in town" is where most of the accidents happen.

Up to 50 percent of parents do not have their children buckle up for in-town driving. This is a scary thought if you trust other parents to drive your child to a birthday party or to Brownie camp. If you're one of those parents, please allow this chapter to inspire you to change.

If you already do buckle your children up, make sure they are in car seats that correctly fit them. The number of car and booster seat alternatives that are available on the market today makes this quite challenging, but it's essential to choose the correct seat for your child.

An NHTSA survey found that a full 72 percent of children were not seated and buckled correctly. Fitting car seats properly is not easy, but it's a disgrace and a tragedy that three-quarters of us cannot get it right when the police hold frequent car seat clinics just to help us learn. It is a disgrace and a tragedy we don't accept their help. I know that it is like some game-show torture to fit a strange car seat into a strange car when we are not even getting the one in our own, familiar car to fit right.

Reality Check

✓ More than 50 percent of child car accident fatalities could be prevented by seat belts. Seat belts are simply the easiest, least expensive way to keep your child alive; they are provided in every car.

Preventative Tips

One out of four vehicle deaths among children from birth to age fourteen involves a driver who has been drinking alcohol. More than two-thirds of these fatally injured children were riding with the drinking driver. This means that it was their parent or designated guardian who was drinking. Although many people think they can hold their liquor, the accident rate shows that they can't. We don't drive after an office party, but we will drive after a kid's party even if we have had a couple of margaritas while watching the kids eat cake. Do not entrust your children to a carpool parent who will have a few drinks at a party and then put your children in the car without a seat belt.

Teen drivers. Once your children can drive themselves, you need to be especially vigilant. High school–age boys are more likely than girls to rarely or never wear seat belts. A full 10 percent never do. Others use them occasionally. Work with your children from a young age so they are in the habit of buckling up. Teenage boys may see going without a seat belt as an act of rebellion. (See the "Boys Versus Girls" section on page 164 for all the dangerous things that boys can do with cars.) Child-safety experts encourage parents to show their teenage boys

photos of teenagers' accidents so they understand the implica-
tions—there is nothing rebellious in those images.

Kids under sixteen. Children under forty pounds should
always ride in car seats. Kids from forty to eighty pounds belong
in booster seats. No matter what the weight of a child, all children should remain in booster seats until they are at least four
feet, nine inches tall. Sitting in the back seat reduces the likelihood of serious injury to children under sixteen years old by a
whopping 40 percent. No matter what the length of the journey
is, always buckle your child up.

Reality Check

✓ If Mom, Dad, and teenage boys would stop drinking and driving,
two-thirds of all car accidents would be prevented.

Parents' Worry Number 2: School Snipers

After the shootings at Columbine and Virginia Tech, we worry
about our kids at school. I worry about my kids, in particular,
since we live in the neighborhood between Columbine and
Lakewood, the scenes of the most-publicized school shootings.

My daughter rushed off the bus last month and exclaimed,
"Mom, you won't believe what happened at school today. We
had a real lockdown. Three guys in hoods came up to the window and knocked on the window with a gun. Our teacher
announced it in a whisper because the bad guys were right there.
He said, 'Remember all we have practiced in the drill.' He said

that this wasn't a drill. We combat-crawled away from the window and hid under the table. Mr. T told us all about Columbine while we lay on our stomachs. Hey, Mom, didn't we go to a Creek-Columbine football game? Could they have shot us if we won? Then the men teachers and the librarian went out to protect the perimeter until the police got there. We couldn't see anything, though, because we had to stay down on the floor."

My daughter, and some other fourth graders, continued recounting more school-sniper details while I and two other moms at the bus stop stood with our mouths hanging open.

"Mom, it's on the TV. We watched it back at lunch."

We grabbed our kids, went to the nearest house, and put on the TV. Nothing. I couldn't reach the school by phone, so I dashed off an e-mail to my daughter's teacher: "Did you just wrestle three gun-toting thugs to the ground?" I asked.

"It was a drill," he texted back.

I am still not 100 percent certain what went on, but it seems this wasn't a normal drill, but a "pretend real" drill meant to make the older kids think it was a real incident. The incident-obsessed fourth graders were reveling in their survival so loudly that they didn't catch the in-school TV announcement about it not having been real, only "pretend real." Fourth-graders have very selective hearing. The lower grades had been locked into their classrooms and told to lie on their tummies for twenty minutes without an explanation.

How many asthma and allergy attacks happened after the twenty-minute lockdown, the kids with their noses in the carpet—

a carpet that is cleaned with the most toxic chemicals imaginable?

We in Colorado may have a history of shootings—three in the last eleven years. But sniper attacks are rare, given the number of schools, the number of students, and the number of school days. Your child is not under day-to-day, minute-by-minute threat of a school sniper. Nor is my child under immediate threat worth every expense to control. Schools are not under siege.

Every time you blink, there's a kid getting hurt in a car accident. But a sniper event is once a year, on the average. A sniper is possible—anything is possible—but an asteroid falling and chipping your windshield is more likely, yet we don't mount laser guns on our cars to blast incoming asteroids.

Mall snipers happen, also rarely. But the mall doesn't have security checks, perimeter fencing, and buzz entry with ID checks. We go to the mall with hardly ever a doubt of our safety. Yet we advocate daily for the safety of our children at school.

These drills and the sniper proofing of schools, like airport security precautions, are to calm parents' and travelers' fears but do not prevent real threats. Scaring kids senseless doesn't stop a disgruntled student from sneaking a gun into the school or a mentally disturbed killer with an agenda and no fear.

What are we doing? We are so panicked about school snipers that we demand all, spend all, and go to ridiculous lengths. Some parents' common sense is so distorted by the worries of sniper kids that they have called the police to turn in their own teens as potential murderers. Their reasons were that they didn't have good relations with their teens. We think that the parents of the Columbine shooters should have known what was going on with them. But every child is not a suspect for parents to fear.

Many principals report that much of their valuable time is taken up with parents who want their child put in the sniper-safest seat in each class. The parents at a school my children used to attend demanded monthly meetings on predators and snipers but no meeting on why the state standardized test scores fell from 97 (excellent) to 67 (extremely poor).

We think that the more money we spend, the more safety we can buy. Wrong.

A local school was convinced to take the entire substitute-teacher budget and the fund for textbooks and new books for the library and use it to pay for a $250,000 plan to sniper proof the school: perimeter fencing; a new entry with two locked-off "holding areas for people visiting the school; closed-circuit TV (CCTV) cameras everywhere; secret classroom intercoms linked to central control; panic buttons; and special windows and doors. The parents initially voted for this. (The project was canceled when the principal was encouraged to find a new school.)

A locked door, everyone who enters being viewed by CCTV or in vision before being buzzed in, and each visitor checking in with the front office to get a visitor's badge are all effective enough. These measures won't stop students from carrying guns, and they won't stop a determined killer, but neither would $250,000 worth of safety equipment.

Basic security works great. Spending more does not solve problems. Not publicizing snipers helps to deter the fame seekers. TV fame is the incentive for some.

Security companies are thriving by offering $100,000 to $500,000 security packages to parents and schools to keep the children safe. Meanwhile, our children will not be prepared to find jobs in this increasingly global economy. The goal of school is education, not Fort Knox–style protection. We know that locking our children into a white padded room to keep them safe from the world is ridiculous (however much we want to keep them safe), but that is exactly what we are doing to our schools: turning them into safes, all locked up, with our children secured inside.

Reality Check

✓ On the average, not even one school a year has a sniper or student-shooter incident.

Preventative Tips

If your school suggests extreme security measures, ask the administration what it wants to accomplish. Schools need to take a sensible approach to school security and follow it: locked doors, CCTV camera, intercom recognition before anyone is buzzed in, and sign in and badges for visitors. It sounds like a lot, but those steps are cheap and effective.

We are politically correct about everything except dangers; for those, we use the scariest words and end up panicking our children. Watch how you talk about remote dangers. Be serious, with gravity, but don't be horrifying.

Replace terrifying sniper drills with an all-inclusive emergency practice. Be smart, and don't scare your children. Most emergencies can be dealt with through the same action plan, so have a general drill for the children. Fires, tornadoes, snipers, and biodisasters are all remote possibilities, but all are served adequately with one general drill.

Tension Tamer:

Remember that school is one of the safest places for your child to be— and that is without sniper proofing.

This general preparedness puts kids in control instead of scaring them with horror scenarios.

Real Danger Number 2: Homicide

The facts sound horrifying: Sixteen kids a day are killed. Kids are killing kids. That was the Christmas season headline in 2009 "from the CDC," the news reports said.

The CDC does list homicide as the number two cause of death for children under seventeen. So the news report was accurate; nevertheless, it's misleading. What the news report said wasn't exactly what the CDC said. The CDC said "sixteen teens and young adults." Most news stories left "young adults" out of the headline, saying "sixteen kids" or "sixteen teens" are killed every day. Since young adults have a much higher violence and crime rate than kids and teens, lumping them together doesn't tell the same story.

Saying "kids" makes all the children in this country seem

threatened. This use of the word *kids* instead of the more accurate *young adults* makes it appear, statistically, that our children are turning into killer kids and that violence will engulf every neighborhood. That is not true. The suburbs are not falling prey to killer kids.

Twelve hundred children under eighteen in this country are dying each year from intentional shootings. It is usually teens from poor areas who are murdering other teens.

Poor, unemployed young adults murdering one another is horrific, but it does not follow that a killer-kid epidemic is spreading to every neighborhood in the nation. Young adult murders require urgent action, but it is different from a world of Uzi-toting eight-year-olds gunning one another down as in a violent video game.

For some high-risk kids and teens, theirs is a nightmare world. Poverty is the major factor, irrespective of race. A poor white child is in as much danger or may resort to violence as much as a poor black or Hispanic child. For certain groups, homicide is the central urgent problem demanding attention and compassion, yet to have 90 percent or more of the parenting population thinking their children could be shot at any moment is craziness on a national level.

The high-risk group in the case of homicide is so specific that general statistics do not show the average national picture. Some advocates paint the tragedy as invading our suburbs, but it is not. Killer kids in all forms are extremely rare. School killers are the rarest.

A thousand deaths confined to a few high-risk neighborhoods

is a tragedy for those areas. But for the majority of parents, homicide is not a danger that should be on their radar. The problem should be fixed by the majority but not contribute to most parents' siege mentality.

There is an easy way to lower the danger. Homicide is usually committed with guns, and guns are also used in robbery and suicide. Kids in the United States are sixteen times more likely to be murdered with a gun, eleven times more likely to commit suicide with a gun, and nine times more likely to die from a gun accident than children in the top twenty-five other industrialized countries combined. In an average year, the number of children who die from being shot is as follows: Japan, 0; Britain, 20; Germany, 60; France, 110; Canada, 150; United States, 5,300.

The other countries have rigid gun control laws. Countries that don't allow guns seldom have many shooting deaths.

More than half of the parents in the United States keep guns. Nearly all of those parents admit to not locking up those guns or to leaving the ammunition with the guns. In fact, most leave their guns unlocked and loaded. Why? How many occasions do we have in which we must grab a gun to defend ourselves? These are supposed to be guns for sport. We lock up our household cleaners; why can't parents lock up their guns?

Preventative Tip

If you have a gun at home, lock it.

Parents' Worry Number 3: Terrorism

One morning, when we still lived in London, I walked my five-year-old to her school, as usual. Some of us moms sat at a street café for a quick sanity-essential, stress-relieving coffee before rushing our kids to the church playgroup. Suddenly the street went eerily quiet. All traffic stopped, and only a few sirens could be heard. London becomes this quiet only when the residents of every home and office are watching the World Cup final; then, the streets are deserted, as if a neutron bomb had exploded.

No one worried until we realized that none of us could get a cell phone signal. The café TV was reporting a power failure on the underground subway system.

Then a woman ran in saying seven underground trains and twenty buses had been blown up by terrorists. We ran a block to the school, but the administrators said we couldn't come in because they were on terrorist lockdown.

One train bomb went off at a station just a block and a half from my daughter's school and the café where I had been sitting at an outdoor table. The explosion had happened just after I dropped her off, while we were ordering our lattes and chatting about our current worries about our kids: the minibully; the bully's mom, who was in denial; and the upcoming bus field trip.

It took all day to get an accurate report. Seven underground trains and two buses had been blown up, killing forty-six.

In your average U.S. small town or suburb, machine gun–toting special forces soldiers in combat suits do not patrol the aisles of the grocery store. But they do in my former local grocery store in London, starting after that terrorist attack and continuing to the present.

One of my London friends had missed her regular bus that day, and that was one of the two buses that was blown up. Since I moved to the United States, my friends here tell me that they live in continual fear of a terrorist attack—far, far more than any of my London friends do (even my friend who missed the bus).

The United States, post-9/11, is a fearful nation in which even people who are personally far removed from the 9/11 tragedy are suffering from post-traumatic stress disorder (PTSD), and they are letting that general paranoia spread to other aspects of their lives and to their families. When a terrorist attack is experienced firsthand, the limited nature of such attacks in the Western world becomes clear: not every store, school, and workplace will be bombed. You realize that most people are safe almost all the time. When such attacks are heard about in the abstract, it is hard to comprehend that *possible* doesn't mean *pervasive*.

Research shows that if the threat of terrorism is properly explained, most children from a stable home environment will not get PTSD, even from an incident as close as the London bombings were to us—two blocks away. But the incidence of PTSD is higher in the Midwest than in New York or Washington, D.C., the front lines of terrorism in the United States. Many of my friends in Colorado are far more fearful than those in London or in lower Manhattan near the World Trade Center.

It is hard not to feel at war against terrorism. We've created an environment of fear. Multicolored alerts at airports, toddlers being asked to hand over teddy bears for the security screening, politicians wanting votes so they can make the country safe, TV wanting to drive up ratings by featuring sensational stories—all these are making us paranoid. Yes, it happened once, and it could happen again. But the fear of random events has more impact on us than any threat deserves.

Paranoia costs lives. Scottish researchers found that 1,700 people who drove instead of taking a plane in the year after 9/11 died in car accidents. Normally, those people would have flown, but their fear of another terrorist attack involving airplanes led them to the real killer, the car.

One mom who consulted with me asked for my help. She had just come back from her vacation with her son. She said that she was so frightened of a terrorist attack on the airplane that she didn't speak to her son during the entire flight. She didn't want to reveal her deep fear—so she said nothing.

Sitting on an airplane, panicked that the plane will be taken down by terrorists is one survey's top worry. The real odds that this will happen, calculated by the CDC, are about 1 in 55 million.

Not talking to her son for hours on a flight could cause more problems for this woman and her child than the chance of a terrorist attack.

Reality Check

✓ You are almost 1,000 times more likely to be struck by lightning than to die in a terrorist attack. You have a 1 in 56,000 chance of getting struck by lightning.

✓ The chance of dying in any sort of terrorist attack has been estimated at 1 in 9 million. Of course, that means it is slightly more likely you will die in an avalanche.

Here are the odds that you will be in a terrorist attack:

- 1 in 88,000, if there were one terrorist attack a week.
- 1 in 1,500,000 at a shopping mall, if there were one terrorist attack a week at shopping malls and you shopped two hours a week.
- 1 in 55,000,000 in an airplane, if there were one terrorist attack a month on planes and you flew once a month.

Real Danger Number 3:
Maltreatment or Abuse

If you want something to be worry about, sexual abuse is it. Yet the perpetrator is usually not who you think it is: it's much more likely to be Great Uncle Joe than a stranger in a Mickey Mouse suit. "Character" perpetrators and strangers are not the norm, so go ahead and book that Disney vacation.

Who are the culprits? It's usually family and friends. But it is taboo in most segments of our society to talk about that. It's not discussed enough, and therefore simple precautions and preventions are discussed even less. Telling your child not to talk to strangers does not keep them safe from most child molesters.

The numbers are staggering: one in four girls and one in six boys report being sexually abused by the time they are eighteen. (These are just the *reported* cases, however.) In most cases, the perpetrators were known to the family. A full one-third of the individuals I spoke to for this book regarding other subjects told me that they had suffered such trauma. The ones who tried to tell other family members were shunned, whereas it should have been the perpetrator who was ostracized and, indeed, arrested.

For babies and toddlers, abuse comes primarily from mothers, so if you know a new mom who is more than usually stressed out, give her some help.

Surprisingly, research confirms that if you warn the people in your life that you would have a perpetrator arrested, family and "friends" are usually deterred from committing abuse. Even knowing this, most people wouldn't feel comfortable sitting down at Christmas dinner with ninety-year-old grandmother and all their aunts, uncles, and cousins and concluding grace with "We thank God for this bountiful meal, and if any of you molest my children, I will drag you screaming through the courts to end your days rotting in prison. So if you are even thinking about abusing my child, know that I will turn you in. Amen."

We should say something like that (though perhaps pick a more suitable time to say it), but we don't. Being forthcoming with a warning would go far in solving the problem. If the one contemplating abuse knows that you will turn him in without hesitation, he will be less inclined to do it. Paranoid Parents suggests a fridge magnet that says "Mess with my kids, and I prosecute." Your kids just think you will stand up for them, whatever happens, and the grown-ups will get the message. Kids probably won't know you are talking about sexual abuse but will see you supporting them in all their troubles. And that message will go a long way to stop the problem before it starts.

Reality Check
✓ Abuse and maltreatment usually happen in the home or in the neighborhood. For school-age kids, the latchkey-kid time of 4:00 to 6:00 PM is overwhelmingly when abuse happens, and it usually happens at home.

Preventative Tips
Telling your child not to talk to strangers does not keep them safe from most child molesters, because the crime is perpetrated most often by a family member or someone known to the family (e.g., coach, teacher, neighbor, or friend).

This devastating crime can often be prevented quite simply. If the abuser thinks that there is even the possibility of being turned in, he (or she) will often stop.

Teach your children that no one touches them, especially their private parts. Doctors and parents are the exception.

Parents' Worry Number 4: Stranger Danger

Stranger danger encompasses both the kidnapping and abuse issues, and it is the parents' (very misguided) plan of action to deal with those imagined and real concerns.

Stranger danger is preached by parents. But not only parents. Somehow law enforcement has gotten involved. I heard an airport security guard checking IDs and tickets say to a little girl, "You look so pretty in your princess dress. I bet I know where you are going. Are you excited? . . . Very good. You shouldn't tell me. I shouldn't have asked you. You know, 'Never talk to strangers.' You are right, I am a stranger. Good girl." Who is this little girl going to turn to if she is lost in an airport if the security guard is a stranger to be feared? And I have heard the same from law enforcement in school classrooms.

We teach our children fear of every stranger, but strangers are the ones who usually help if our children get lost—and they do get lost, a lot. More than 2,000 children get lost in this country every day, on average. They wander off at the beach, in the store, and at the playground, or they miss the school bus. Much of the time, they are returned by strangers.

At our child-care center, the teachers talked about stranger danger once a week, causing me to have to calm a set of very frightened triplets.

Kids have become indoctrinated with the stranger danger message to the point of phobia. We hear so often fearful children demanding of mom who is talking to the check-out person at the store or the plumber, "Mom, stop talking to that stranger! Why were you talking to them, they're strangers." They feel parents are doing something "life and death" wrong and are very frightened.

So why have strangers gotten such a bad rap?

Strangers are the unknown, and we fear the unknown. We can't control strangers, and we can't quantify or judge what we can't control. Strangers do rarely commit random bad acts, but because people can't cope with randomness, such acts seem more frightening than nonrandom acts. Since we can't control random crimes, we grossly overinflate their danger. The lack of control and predictability so freaks us out that we perceive those dangers as about a thousand or even a million times worse than truly dangerous but familiar events (which we often deny exist—family abuse and car accidents being the most obvious).

We need to teach skills to escape *known* predators.

Reality Check

✓ Only .004 percent of kidnappings are perpetrated by a stranger. The maltreatment of infants and toddlers is usually committed by the parents and guardians. Abuse is most often committed by family members, "friends," and acquaintances. Even murder is usually perpetrated by someone you know.

Preventative Tips

Children should never approach a car when a driver asks for information or asks them to get in, regardless of whether they know the person.

Teach your child different scenarios, such as avoiding some-one who is asking for help finding a lost dog or cat, and never to go alone anywhere without asking you first.

A secret code system in which only the child and parent-approved adults know the code word does not always work for children under six. Far too often, very young children give away the secret word immediately, proud that they remembered it. Clear sign-in and sign-out procedures at school or day care, strictly monitored by the staff, is essential.

Teach children the correct actions that apply to *all* people, strangers or familiar: not approaching cars, what to do when lost, knowing their parents' phone numbers.

Teach the difference between bad touch and good touch. Don't frighten children to the point that they are living with a perpetual fear of strangers.

Remember: the likelihood is great that the child and the family will know the predator.

Real Danger Number 4: Suicide

Suicide is a true danger that should be on the radar of parents, especially parents of boys. Whereas suicide accounts for 1.2 percent of all deaths in the United States annually, it accounts for 12.8 percent of all deaths among fifteen- to twenty-four-year-olds. In the age group fifteen to nineteen, teen boy "successful" suicides total nearly 1,700, but teen girl suicides numbered only about 350.

What makes teens suicidal? Teen brain development lessens

their ability to read people's faces. They have difficulty understanding what others are trying to convey. This can make relating to the world difficult and frustrating. Teens often feel isolated. Separating from parents and making mistakes is frustrating. A system for prioritizing what is important now versus what will be important in the future may not be developed in some teens. Self-esteem is almost totally derived from appearance rather than accomplishments. This means that they can have straight As or make the varsity soccer team but still be depressed if they have a bad hair day. The social power struggle is a daily roller coaster. Drug and alcohol experimentation doesn't help, either.

Teens are moody, but often they are not talking to you simply because they are making crude attempts at independence. It can be extremely difficult to tell what is normal teen behavior and what is suicidal behavior.

Reality Check

✓ Suicide is the third leading cause of death for young people (ages fifteen to twenty-nine).

✓ There are 12 suicides for every 100,000 adolescents.

✓ Approximately twelve young people between the ages of fifteen and twenty-four commit suicide every day.

Preventative Tips

Know that boys and young men may not make a series of suicide attempts before succeeding. Boys usually choose suicide methods that succeed immediately: guns and hanging. Guns are at the neighbor's or the friend's house, so teaching resilience is the only true defense.

Typically, girls attempt but rarely succeed. Girls choose pills or try to slit their wrists. These methods are convenient for them but also take the longest, thus giving the best opportunity to be rescued. Monitor girls' Internet activity to get a clue to the girls' state of mind. Most suicides happen in the child's home during the home-alone time of after school to early evening. Avoid the latchkey experience by planning after-school activities. If you are worried about your children's distance and unresponsiveness, seek outside help.

If you are paying the Internet and phone bills and you are really worried about your children, you may look at their texts and Internet activity. Just try to act on it only if it is truly a life-and-death situation. Connect with your kids through family dinners and activities. Keep talking to your children and showing interest in them even if they don't respond.

Teach perspective from an early age. Teach kids to look back and see where they have triumphed and how adversity has ended. No one had ever pointed out to the Columbine perpetrators that in a few days they would graduate, be on their way to college, and never see their tormentors (fellow students) again.

Connect with your children physically. Not hugging boys doesn't make them better men; it makes them socially disconnected, which is exactly what you want to avoid. Hug your sons and your daughters forever.

Don't reward defeat. Avoid giving a "poor you" message by

rewarding defeat with hugs and lavish attention; this can begin a cycle of self-pity. Especially with sports, losing should not be seen as failure so losing needs no consoling. The motto should be: it is not whether you win or lose, it is fun to play the game. Teach "Don't stress the small stuff, and everything is the small stuff."

Reality Check

✓ In a typical high school classroom, probably three students (one boy and two girls) have made a suicide attempt in the past year. Almost 20 percent of high-school students have stated on self-report surveys that they have seriously considered attempting suicide during the preceding twelve months. Guns are the most common method among youths, used in three of five completed suicides. Research has shown that access to firearms is a significant factor in the rate of youth suicide.

Parents' Worry Number 5: Drugs

Pushers on the playground, eight-year-old drug dealers—these are not news stories, these are story lines from TV crime shows. They are not the norm.

There is good news—and it's about drugs! Most high schoolers think that using drugs is stupid. They really do. I am not saying that the prevention of drug abuse is a cause that gets too much funding; I am saying that kids are on board more than we think and that the message, for the most part, is getting through.

Recent research shows that most teens think that drug use and even most drug experimentation are dangerous, stupid, and something they would not do. Some teens will experiment sometimes. They are experimenting with levels of what is reasonable and what isn't. They say that they might try pot or ecstasy once, but more than once or twice is considered stupid. Very few become habitual offenders, be it with drugs, gambling, crime, or other overreported vices that supposedly make teens today the worst of any generation. It is usually the same "bad" kid who is trying multiple drugs, having sex, binge drinking, and cutting school.

Our teens are *not* the worst. They are *not* in the most danger of any teenagers ever. All generations think that their teens are going down the road to society's destruction. But the statistics paint a completely different picture than the media paints.

In an anonymous survey, eight out of ten adults said that drug abuse has never been a problem in their family. They say that their fears come from the media, not from personal experience. We are paranoid without any personal experience.

Reality Check

✓ The antidrug campaigns that start early with young children at school are working. A problem is that with each generation, the antidrug campaign goes after the drugs that have been the most dangerous at that time.

✓ Each generation has its drug of choice. Right now the news is getting out there that drugs like heroin, methamphetamine, and cocaine are not okay to try. Teens get that. Now the publicity must increase about prescription drugs and the abuse of cough syrups and the like, without losing the message of avoiding harder drugs.

✓ Poor kids and rich kids are most at risk for a drug habit. For poor kids, drugs are an escape. Rich kids have the money to experiment. Again, keep in mind that one "wild" kid will try numerous drugs, and that skews the statistics.

Preventative Tips

Demanding but not explaining total abstinence has proved ineffective for drugs, sex, or any vice. "No" without an explanation is like a red flag to a bull. Substitute a discussion for "No! Never!"

Preaching abstinence without providing accurate information can undermine your message. Teens will see other teens doing recreational drugs with little lasting effect and think that you lied to them when you said (or implied) that all drugs are equally bad. If you lied, you have given them permission, in their minds, to throw out the entire "Just say no" message. They will find out for themselves, and that can mean experimentation. Pot is not as dangerous as meth in terms of addiction, but smoking pot and then driving could be just as dangerous as doing cocaine. Smoking pot at a party is not as dangerous as doing heroin.

This is not to say that it's okay to try recreational drugs. It means that it is important to give kids accurate, objective knowledge that they can use to judge the temptations that will be put in their way. Your kids need this information as soon as they are old enough for those discussions.

If your kids are well educated, then by and large, they will make the right drug choices. Teens often think that their parents do not listen to them, so talk to them like the responsible kids that most of them are. Compliment them for the smart choices they are learning to make.

Have an older cousin or an older neighborhood kid whom your children admires come and chat with them about tough subjects like friendship and bullying, drugs and sex, and suicide. The older kid can relay the message that the younger kids will get through these complicated times and can explain how to cope.

Real Danger Number 5:
Unintentional Drowning

For most children, swimming pools are a bigger danger than guns. Stephen Dubner and Steven Levitt, the authors of *Freakonomics: A Rogue Economist Explores the Hidden Side of Everything*, brilliantly drew attention to this fact. Some parents won't let their children go to a house where there are guns, but they let their children go to a house with a swimming pool. Their children are far more likely to be hurt or even die in the swimming pool than with the guns.

Why do so many children drown? A giant tsunami doesn't pull them under, nor does the Loch Ness Monster swallow them. The cause is lack of parental supervision.

This is an example of when hovering is okay. Watch your kids! Some parents try a "tag team" approach when they are at the pool with friends: they designate a different parent each ten minutes to be the "parent on watch." The two times I tried that, it resulted in near disasters. One dad forgot that he was to watch the kids, and he got into the hot tub to read his newspaper. His son fell in the deep end of the pool and was rescued by the lifeguard.

On another occasion, a mother said she'd watch my triplets while I got the life jackets from the car. Within one minute, my five-year-old daughter fell in the pool and panicked, even though she could almost touch the bottom with her feet. She went under several times, and I had to jump in and pull her out. Watching means watching *every second*. That mom had mistakenly assumed that my daughter could swim as well as her daughter could when she was that age.

When you are around children and water, this is a time to be justifiably vigilant. Don't have a false sense of security because there are lifeguards. For example, when we moved into a neighborhood that had a community pool, several parents warned me that the lifeguards were nice girls but that they texted while lifeguarding. All three of those parents had previously had to jump in the pool fully clothed to rescue their kids that season.

Whatever applies to the swimming pool also applies to the bathtub. Bathing should be a chaperoned activity every moment; just don't use life jackets. Don't use bath seats, either; they make it easier for parents to hold children while they're bathing them, but they are not devices for leaving children alone.

Pediatric authorities and consumer agencies want all bath seats banned. As with much childproofing, parents are lulled into a false sense of security that their child is safe by buying some "miracle" safety device. However, bath safety means that you are there watching your babies and toddlers *every second*.

Reality Check

✓ Of all the children who will die this year, more than one-quarter will drown. That's approximately 1,125 deaths a year. Five times as many children *nearly* drown each year. They survive, but often with brain damage. Three-quarters of the victims are boys. We teach our boys to be macho, so they think shouting for help is something they just should not do. Sometimes they don't shout for help because they think they will get in trouble. We need to reconsider how we prepare our little boys for accidents, because our culture's approach to preparing boys for life is killing them. Home pools are the usual location of most of these drownings. In the usual scenario, the children will be out of their parents' sight for only a couple of minutes, but that is enough time to wander off and drown.

Preventative Tips

Don't be fooled by the advertising. Only coast guard–certified life jackets can keep your little nonswimmer from drowning. Floaties, noodles, inner tubes, and buoyancy suits will *not* stop your child from drowning.

Don't expect too much from your children in regard to swimming. The average child cannot coordinate the crawl until he or she is five years old.

I can't stress this message too much: teach little boys that it's okay—even desirable—to cry for help.

Working pool gates are a must. Also, you can buy a device for your home pool that sounds an alert if the surface of the water is broken.

If you are watching your kids at a pool and need to go to the bathroom, or one of your little ones needs a potty trip, don't leave your kids in the pool. They just have to get out of the pool and wait at the side or, better yet, come with you. (And it's a good idea to have "everyone try" while you're there, so you aren't constantly going to the restroom.)

Don't just sit poolside reading a book or a magazine while you are on pool duty.

Save tryouts for the swim team until your children can really swim. A swim team should not take any child until he or she can easily swim a length.

You teach your child not to run into the street to chase a ball. The same applies to toys that fall into the pool. Only Mom or Dad goes after the ball that has fallen in.

Enforce the rule that no one swims alone—ever. Even when children are older and in a crowded pool, they should swim with buddies.

Parents' Worry Number 6: Vaccinations

Our grandparents and great grandparents can remember the little children's coffins during the measles, mumps, and rubella epidemics. In 1964, rubella killed 11,000 fetuses, and 20,000 babies were born prematurely and permanently disabled when their pregnant mothers were exposed. Twelve million people contracted rubella. Before vaccination, 3 to 4 million people got measles; about 400 a year died, and a huge number were left with chronic disabilities.

The diseases have been almost eliminated in the United States . . . for now. Worldwide, 450 children died every day last year from measles; that's about 164,000 deaths. According to the WHO, there were 733,000 measles deaths in the year 2000.

What caused the number of deaths to reduce so dramatically? Vaccination.

The value of vaccinations is one of the clear-cut scientifically proven truths in modern medicine today. But the epidemics will be back if we don't look at the facts about vaccinations and dispel some of the myths that have arisen. So why are children not being vaccinated? Why are we seeing mini-epidemics in some areas of the country? Parents have been scared off from vaccinating by sensationalized-hearsay stories that vaccinations cause autism.

A small group of highly distraught parents is looking for an answer to the rapidly increasing rate of children's autism, which is understandable. Like parents of kidnapped and murdered children, the parents of autistic children are very vocal and very persuasive in their attempts to help other parents. Being a passionate parent trying to help other parents is noble. But the problem is that there is no proven link between vaccinations and autism. Yet it remains the parents' firm belief. Their panic is infectious and panics all parents. Many parents don't know what to do so they do nothing—which means they are not vaccinating their children.

The autism-vaccination link wouldn't hold up in court, because the evidence is entirely circumstantial. Autism seems connected to vaccinations because autism starts to appear at the same time that children are vaccinated with the measles, mumps, and rubella (MMR) vaccine. Doctors are getting better at diagnosing autism, and the criteria for what constitutes autism have been increased. Thus, it appears that the autism rate has gone up with the start of the MMR vaccinations.

No substantiated, properly performed studies have ever shown any link to autism whatsoever. Here are the details of the one study "proving" the autism/MMR vaccine link. It was conducted on twelve children. It took place eight years after the children were vaccinated. The evidence was what the children's parents remembered about the symptoms eight years earlier. The doctor made the claim of the link and became very famous and rich. It was later shown that the lawyers for some of the parents paid the doctor large sums of money to make the claim (presumably to file huge financial claims against the vaccine manufacturers). In England's *Guardian* newspaper on February 2, 2010, Richard Horton, the editor of the medical journal that published the research, said he realized that "It was utterly clear, without any ambiguity at all, that the statements in the paper were utterly false." Huge international studies involving countless children

WORRY LESS TIP:

Don't vaccinate your children when they are sick or have a fever; wait until they are well. Parents can do individual inoculations instead of the combined MMR, but it is easy to forget to do all and even harder to remember the boosters. To worry less, vaccinate. Epidemics kill tens of thousands and disable hundreds of thousands. Vaccinations have been cleared of the autism charge.

have never shown a link between autism and MMR vaccinations. But a study of twelve children involving bribes, falsified information, and no scientific method was shouted out louder than the truth.

Billions have been spent on comprehensive, sound medical tests by governments worldwide, not just the U.S. government. World health organizations are now refusing to spend their money on more tests to prove or disprove an autism-vaccination link. They say that a disproportionate amount of money has been spent that proves the same thing: there is no autism-vaccination connection. The authorities now see such research as a waste of funds. Enormous amounts of money could have been spent to cure or treat autism; instead, these funds have been wasted on proving no link in test after test after test.

The medical profession cannot understand how such clear-cut, totally sound proof can be discounted by so much of the general public. *Discover* magazine named the proof the number one discovery of the year. The magazine also said that it is a major national tragedy that the proof is not accepted by many in the general population. The editors believe that a real, not hyped, genuine health crisis is coming because parents have started turning away from vaccinations. Some areas of the country have already had mini-epidemic outbreaks.

I could not feel more sympathy for the suffering parents and their lovely children, but the nation does not need an epidemic of any sort.

Reality Check

✓ The nation will be at risk if vaccinations do not become the norm again. Mothers, do you want your unvaccinated child to get mumps when you are carrying the new brother or sister? Dads need to be advocates for vaccination too.

Real Danger Number 6: Fire

Of all the fire deaths in the nation, more than a third have been of children under five. Two-thirds of those children were black. More little boys than girls have died.

About 630 children under the age of twenty die every year from fire or flame injuries. These are 630 deaths that should have never happened. The "good" news is that fire-related deaths are almost 100 percent preventable. The fixes are so easy.

Reality Check

✓ Half of the residences where fire deaths and injuries happened did *not* have fire alarms or smoke detectors, which tells you something about prevention. Almost all fires involve cigarette smoking, which is the main cause of all fire deaths.

Poverty is also a factor. Bad wiring and sealed or barred basement windows are lethal for small children. Cheap portable heaters can be a real danger, too. This is compounded by parents being unable to afford smoke detectors.

In many cases, little boys do not get out when there is a fire because they don't want to shout for help. See the section on drowning (page 74) for why this is so.

Preventative Tips

Smoke alarms save lives. Have working smoke alarms. Check the batteries as recommended. Make sure that fire exits and escape windows aren't blocked or too hard for a child to open. Teach your kids, especially little boys, the escape route in case of a fire. Statistics show that more little boys hide in a fire rather than try to escape. Do fire drills. But remember that a real fire is very different from the motions we go through in a drill.

A Personal Experience

We had just moved into our house in Colorado, and I hadn't yet had time to buy fire extinguishers. I had put some olive oil in a skillet on the stove to heat and had turned away for a minute when my preschool son Zach came into the room and said very calmly, "Mom, the kitchen is on fire. I am taking the others to the backyard." The pan had flames shooting to the ceiling, and the microwave oven above the stove was melting hot plastic. I knew not to throw flour or water onto an oil fire because it would turn the pan into a bomb, so I tried to turn off the burner, but I couldn't get near the stove because of the flames.

The alarm was blaring. *Dumb me, dumb kitchen fire.* Head count in the backyard; I was missing a triplet. The noise was so loud that I couldn't think, and I didn't want the fire department to see what an idiot I was, so I turned off the smoke alarm so I could yell at Abby to get out. We couldn't find her; she was upstairs somewhere. I couldn't leave the kitchen burning and go to find her, because one of my other kids might decide to come in and look, too. Or worse yet, they could try to put out the fire.

The flame had completely died down, so I decided to remove the pan from the burner. I thought that I had better make doubly sure that the house and everyone in it would be safe. *I was being a paranoid parent who had to fix everything.* I hadn't been able to turn the knob before, so I forgot to try again. The handle of the pan was cool, so I picked up the pan.

It burst into flames. I decided to drop it, calculating that there was little grease left in it. That would have worked out okay, except that the pan handle hit the cupboard, which sent the pan down at an angle, which caused the remaining oil to splash on my legs. Luckily, I was not in polyester pants; they would have gone up in flames and melted onto my body. I was in a cotton dress.

I looked down and saw that my legs were on fire. My legs were literally on fire. Oddly, it didn't hurt.

Abby wandered down the stairs. She thought that the alarm was just going off again as it always did when toast burned. I said, "Mommy is hurt." I knew that I needed to go to the hospital, so I got the kids in the car, but I didn't know where the nearest hospital was because we had just moved there.

I had second-degree, nearly third-degree, burns from the knees down. Here I was, the most paranoid and prepared parent in the world, and I really, really could have died from those leg burns. There was a high danger of infection that would require a six-month hospital stay, or worse. Needless to say, I cared for my injured legs well, and it was agonizing. The experience taught me that I should have been more prepared and less prepared at the same time.

Prepared means that if there is a fire, any kind of fire, just get everyone out and call the fire department.

Preventative Tips

Mentally prepare for a real fire scenario when you're doing a fire drill; don't just go through the motions. The kids need to know more than that there are a couple of exits in your home. They need to know what to do in different situations: if there's a hot door, smoke, a grease fire, or a toaster fire. Don't scare them; just teach them how to stay calm and in control when things seem scary.

Call the fire department for every fire. Call the fire department for every smell of burning. Call the fire department for smoke. Call the fire department even if a small fire has been put out. It's their job. They have equipment that can tell them if there is heat behind the walls. Flames can be burning in the walls, and you can't see them.

Get everyone out, regardless of how small the fire is! It is not worth losing your life or your kids' lives.

Never ignore a smoke alarm. (Sort out the burned toast and flambéing false alarms by finding a smoke alarm accurate enough to not go off for a whiff of smoke, or place it at an appropriate distance from the toaster.)

The "stop, drop, and roll" drill is great practice and great advice for avoiding the smoke inhalation that causes most fire deaths. This is the technique to drop to the ground and roll if a person's clothes have caught on fire, but it also helps little ones focus, distracts them from panicking, and gets them to the floor under the smoke during a fire. But many little kids erroneously think that all they need to do is to stop, drop, and roll; they misunderstand and don't realize that their main goal in a fire is to get out of the house.

Most little boys just "stop" and then hide. Teach little boys that it's okay to yell for help. They are afraid that they will get in trouble if they shout for help. They may worry that they aren't being brave. Teach boys to get out!

Once the kids are out of the house, they should call 9-1-1. Be sure that you teach this number to them as nine-one-one. If you say *nine-eleven*, many children will push the nine button, then look for a number eleven and not know what to do when they don't find it.

Buy practical housewarming gifts for new home owners: fire extinguishers, smoke alarms, and carbon-dioxide monitors.

Parents' Worry Number 7:
Playing in the Front Yard or Walking to School

In our polls, we have parents worried about kidnapping again—but this time they worry about strangers lurking around the home, in the neighborhood, and at school, and this is different from the fear of strangers in the "outside" world. Because parents' judgment about kidnapping is so warped, dealing with the home front is important. This fear is crippling independence and the sense of security in our children. It is even affecting their health.

Drop-off at many schools takes a good twenty minutes. It is a testimony of caring, paranoid parents. Too many cars are dropping off children. But what takes the extra time is that all the parents (many of whom are dads on the way to work), wait parked or double-parked while their not-so-little fifth grader walks up the path, up the steps, and inside the door. I do it, too, with a tinge of worry, separation anxiety, and love, as my children walk less than twenty-five feet to the door, clearly in my sight every step of the way.

What is going to happen to a child between the car and the school door? A kindie, that is, a kindergartner, might have trouble opening the door, but there are a dozen big kids there to help. We just love watching—admit it. But for some reason we have it in our minds that a stranger will pop out of the one straggly bush to snatch our child, in front of the other ten parents who are watching vigilantly from their cars and the twenty other parents in cars who are waiting to get into the drop-off zone.

If we won't let our children walk a dozen feet into the school building, we would never mentally and emotionally survive their walking a couple of blocks to school. We even accompany our children to the bus stop, even though the bus stop is less than a block away, in clear sight of our front door. What kind of independence and safety are we teaching?

In many European countries, it is the norm for kindergartners to walk to school on their own, sometimes with their friends and sometimes alone. Babies are left at home sleeping in their cribs while the mother runs an older child to school on a snowy day or goes to the grocery store. In India, the average child can walk home from up to twelve miles away, knowing each and every road in a twelve-mile radius by heart. My brother confessed to me that he used to ride his bike twenty miles across a bridge into another state to buy illegal fireworks. I used to ride my bike ten miles to the mall, yet I didn't let my children ride their bikes three doors down without watching their every move.

In our last neighborhood, the parents had an elaborate calling system in which they phoned one another upon the arrival of each child and phoned when each child was walking home. That sounds great, but our four backyards met together at the back— so the children were just walking from one backyard to an adjoining backyard.

If you are in the middle of a nasty divorce and think that your spouse, who has no visitation rights, will snatch the kids, then it is most likely that he or she, or a new girlfriend or boyfriend as an accomplice, will snatch them from the front yard. Under those circumstances, you are not paranoid about not letting your children play in the front yard.

Otherwise we are scaring our kids again. Kids need to know not to go up to any car, whether it's driven by a stranger or a friend. But there isn't an ever-present stranger lurking in your neighborhood. The fitness level for our children suffers from always riding to school. Walking and biking are great exercise that would benefit our kids daily.

Reality Check

✓ Approximately seven children a year are snatched by a complete stranger from their neighborhoods or front yards. That is 7 out of 74 million. At some point you have to give up your paranoia of everything.

Real Danger Number 7: Suffocation

I hate balloons. Even though they look like an economic, fun child's toy, I am just now letting my kids—ages seven and nine—blow up balloons. And I still think they are too young when I see what they do with balloons, such as trying to blow up the broken bits of exploded balloons. Instead of blowing out, my children suck the balloon in. Sometimes I feel paranoid believing that I must supervise them playing with balloons, as if they were playing with recently sharpened knives. Razor blades versus plastic bags—similar? Believe it or not, more kids die in balloon incidents than razor blade incidents.

READER/CUSTOMER CARE SURVEY

We care about your opinions! Please take a moment to fill out our online Reader Survey at **http://survey.hcibooks.com.**

As a **"THANK YOU"** you will receive a **VALUABLE INSTANT COUPON** towards future book purchases

as well as a **SPECIAL GIFT** available only online! Or, you may mail this card back to us.

(PLEASE PRINT IN ALL CAPS)

First Name _____ MI. _____ Last Name _____

Address _____ City _____

State _____ Zip _____ Email _____

1. Gender
- ☐ Female   ☐ Male

2. Age
- ☐ 8 or younger
- ☐ 9-12   ☐ 13-16
- ☐ 17-20   ☐ 21-30
- ☐ 31+

3. Did you receive this book as a gift?
- ☐ Yes   ☐ No

4. Annual Household Income
- ☐ under $25,000
- ☐ $25,000 - $34,999
- ☐ $35,000 - $49,999
- ☐ $50,000 - $74,999
- ☐ over $75,000

5. What are the ages of the children living in your house?
- ☐ 0 - 14   ☐ 15+

6. Marital Status
- ☐ Single
- ☐ Married
- ☐ Divorced
- ☐ Widowed

7. How did you find out about the book?
(please choose one)
- ☐ Recommendation
- ☐ Store Display
- ☐ Online
- ☐ Catalog/Mailing
- ☐ Interview/Review

8. Where do you usually buy books?
(please choose one)
- ☐ Bookstore
- ☐ Online
- ☐ Book Club/Mail Order
- ☐ Price Club (Sam's Club, Costco's, etc.)
- ☐ Retail Store (Target, Wal-Mart, etc.)

9. What subject do you enjoy reading about the most?
(please choose one)
- ☐ Parenting/Family
- ☐ Relationships
- ☐ Recovery/Addictions
- ☐ Health/Nutrition
- ☐ Christianity
- ☐ Spirituality/Inspiration
- ☐ Business Self-help
- ☐ Women's Issues
- ☐ Sports

10. What attracts you most to a book?
(please choose one)
- ☐ Title
- ☐ Cover Design
- ☐ Author
- ☐ Content

TAPE IN MIDDLE; DO NOT STAPLE

NO POSTAGE
NECESSARY
IF MAILED
IN THE
UNITED STATES

BUSINESS REPLY MAIL
FIRST-CLASS MAIL PERMIT NO 45 DEERFIELD BEACH, FL

POSTAGE WILL BE PAID BY ADDRESSEE

Health Communications, Inc.
3201 SW 15th Street
Deerfield Beach FL 33442-9875

FOLD HERE

Comments

Reality Check

✓ Balloons and shopping bags are a major suffocation danger for little kids. Consumer agencies suggest that balloons be banned. I am not paranoid, but I believe that balloons, like fireworks, require supervision, age-appropriate interaction, and instruction.

✓ Black children under five are at the highest risk of accidents with balloons or plastic shopping bags, and black boys are slightly more at risk than black girls. The rate of death by suffocation from balloons and plastic bags is nearly 1 in 10,000, which is a frighteningly high rate.

✓ Another major cause of suffocation is crib death and similar suffocation. A practice comes and goes of having the newborn baby sleep in the family bed with mom and dad. Or we often drift off to sleep in a chair or on the sofa napping with the baby while we are holding them. These are just not worth the risk. Suffocation does happen in these instances often enough to make it worth not doing.

Preventative Tips

Have a cuddle or a snuggle, but put the baby down in his own crib on his or her back to sleep.

We all dream of the perfect baby bedroom, with a crib decked out with frilly pink or blue pillows, matching quilts and blankets, bed skirts, mobiles, curtains, and plush toys. Get rid of it all. The baby can roll over and suffocate or strangle in all of them. As a bonus, you will save yourselves between $200 and $2,000.

Get rid of window blind cords.

Get a crib with bars no more than two and three-eighths

inches apart (the diameter of a soda can). Don't use a drop-sided crib.

Keep plastic bags, dry-cleaning bags, and balloons away from young children.

Parents' Worry Number 8: Bullying

Parents list bullying as a top concern for their children. Bullying may be even higher than number eight on parents' lists of worries by the time you read this book. News coverage of this topic was unrelenting lately when a fifteen-year-old girl committed suicide after months of constant bullying (and sexual abuse.) Before that, the horrific story of the student set alight by bullies actually prompted our high school parents to demand an information meeting so this would never happen in our school.

I am totally opposed to writing about high-profile cases. It is irresponsible for me to concentrate on the horrors of these stories for several reasons. This book is about important dangers that could happen to your child. This type of bullying is extremely rare. Commenting on cases that have not yet come to trial and with insufficient evidence is not ethical. The occurrence of these cases is not on the increase, but the coverage and exploitation of these cases is on the increase. I am saying the *danger* is not significant. I am *not* saying that these young lives were not significant.

Abusive texting and cyberbullying are so new that comprehensive study statistics are not yet available. But the data, so far, suggests that although it takes place, kids are handling it well. It is promoting fear to say that bullying, which used to take place only in school, now takes place after school. Kids know, and parents can always remind them, it takes active participation (reading the message) to be cyberbullied. Kids can "delete" cyber and text bullying with one click, and that is all it deserves. It is hard not to want to read what others are saying about you, but that is what kids need to learn to do. And evidence shows that is how they are coping with this cyberphenomenon.

Although some of us may have an extreme reaction to the horror stories, what concerns most parents are the "I was bullied" stories that come home daily. Knowledge of the likelihood of bullying can help us.

What is bullying? Parents can become very agitated by some playground talk. A bossy little six-year-old girl nagging an innocent five-year-old boy for not standing perfectly still in line sounds like bullying but is actually normal, acceptable confrontation. What constitutes real bullying? When talk turns into action? How long do we let verbal conflict or harassment go on before we step in to mediate? How far can bullied kids go to defend themselves? What can and should bystanders do to help?

We worry about the safety and happiness of our children at school, where they are beyond our help. In fact, although bullying, school shootings, and hostage taking seem to dominate the news, schools are one of the safest places for your children to be. It will surprise most parents to learn that most children report being happy at school, in spite of the grumbling they may do to you. If they talk about a bully bothering them, be sure to find out the facts and take appropriate action. A long-term study found that most children will never be seriously bullied. Extreme violence is rare. I am not being dismissive about bullying. These are strong statistics.

Reality Check

✓ In a class of thirty sixth-grade students, half, or fifteen, will not be bullied, seven or eight will be bullied once or twice, three will be bullied sometimes, and four will be bullied weekly. By the time most kids are in tenth grade, bullying is not as bad. Of a class of thirty tenth-grade students, twenty-one won't be bullied, five will be bullied once or twice a term, two will be bullied sometimes, and two will be bullied weekly.

The Bullied Child Profile

Most children who are bullied share many similar characteristics:

- They feel extremely lonely.
- They find making friends to be difficult or extremely difficult.
- They feel that they don't have a positive relationship with their classmates.
- They feel they don't fit in.
- They have high levels of insecurity, anxiety, depression and unhappiness, and low self-esteem.
- They have poor psychosocial functioning.
- The boys tend to be physically weaker than their peers.

The parents of a student who is being bullied tend to help out at school, possibly because they are there to protect the child they already know needs protecting. Alternatively, the child isn't fitting in because he is spending time with the parent and not with his classmates. Most bullied children will say that they "don't fit in." Volunteering in elementary school is fine. For girls to see the mother working in the class builds self-esteem. But stop by middle school. Older kids don't want, need, or benefit from their parents being present in any capacity, even if they are sometimes picked on.

The Bully Profile

Most children who bully have at least some of the following characteristics:

- They are more likely to experiment with alcohol and smoking.
- They go to schools that have bad atmospheres.
- They get into fights frequently.
- They have poor psychosocial functioning.
- They have conduct problems.
- They tend to hate school.
- They find making friends to be easy.
- They are not lonely.
- They have a fairly positive relationship with their classmates, who gravitate to powerful children.

Real bullies are the kids who usually become criminals as

adults. Sixty percent of former bullies have criminal records by the time they turn twenty-four, and 35 to 40 percent of them have three or more convictions.

In the real world, bullying feels different than it sounds in the statistics. Kids have conflicts. Most schools have great bully action plans. Mild conflicts can seem overwhelming for a child and worse to the parent. I am hugely frustrated about the policy of my children's school, which I would describe as "no-fault" bullying. The administrators talk to both children and find out what the victim did to "provoke" the hit or kick. Then, because of confidentiality, the administrators will not tell you what, if any, disciplinary steps are being taken. Yes, at least at our school, they won't even tell you the name of a student who is bullying your child—if your child hasn't already told you. Nor will they tell the bully's parents that it is your child who their child is bullying. Total confidentiality is always preserved at our school.

I was very frustrated that my daughter, who was kicked in the eye by a bully, was seen as the instigator because she was swinging her legs as she sat and inadvertently bumped the boy. She said she was sorry, but he got up on the bus seat and kicked her in the face. Nevertheless, she started it, the principal told me, and so she was also at fault. This was even a boy who already had a written record of bullying (and you must make sure the complaint is recorded). Although I love my daughter's school and its administrators, they—like many other school administrators— seem to sacrifice all common sense to protocol. To the parent like me, the principal's response, in positively supporting both children involved, was frustrating. And I am sure she realized how ridiculous and unjust she sounded blaming my child as having a part in being kicked in the eye. How administrators are allowed to mediate can result in Kafka-esque nonsense. But the principal's actions behind the scenes were effective. She could not tell me, but the child's parents were called in (a volunteer parent told me). And fortunately, there have been no more incidents.

So make sure you understand your school's policy on bullying. Keep your cool amid school red tape and procedures, even when it seems that the bully is being enabled and the good kids are getting the blame. You must persevere in the face of bureaucratic procedures.

If there continues to be a problem, get proof, because the authorities will want evidence; then consult the district supervisor. How do you get proof? The proof should consist of photographs and statements from *adult* witnesses. Make sure to create a long paper trail. Document everything and demand that the school keep a file.

Remember, hitting is criminal assault (not at age four or five, of course, but for older children). If you have witnesses and more action is warranted, you can go to the police.

Low-level bullying is a dilemma that statistics don't answer. It used to be considered common sense that adults didn't mediate until bullying became physical rather than merely verbal. It is tough beyond belief not to step in when your child's best friend says something hurtful like "You aren't my friend anymore"— but that's not bullying. The chances are that your child will use that line, too, someday; and eventually both kids will learn that this isn't something you should say unless you really do intend to end the friendship. Your child will learn that a real friend doesn't say things like that. A thick skin can't be bought by parents; it has to be learned the hard way.

If it's difficult for you to ask your kid what's going on, or if your child doesn't want to answer, ask his or her siblings, friends, or friends' parents. I regret to say that I was told by my daughter's friend's *parents* that the bruises on my daughter's legs came from her "best friend" kicking her whenever my daughter played with other girls.

Preventative Tips

Tension Tamer:

Statistics indicate that most kids love school most of the time. Some of the most successful and famous people were bullied. Your child may experience some bullying, but he or she can still have a great life outside and beyond school.

Go through the school instead of confronting a parent directly. Don't mediate on behalf of other upset parents. I meddled for another upset mom and lost my friend for awhile because she was in denial that her daughter was bullying.

Martial arts can be effective for both self-esteem and self-defense without involving any direct violence.

Get your bullied child involved with activities or kids outside school; he or she will see that there is life outside the school hierarchy.

Help your child bond with other kids

by having playdates. Focus on goals, schoolwork, activities, and a strong family life. Undermine the extreme peer pressure to conform by pointing out good role models and a healthy respect for differences.

Be prepared for a frustrating time.

Real Danger Number 8: Bicycle Accidents

There are only 193 bicycle deaths a year of children and young adults up to age twenty. That is a low number. When our real eighth danger takes only 193 children a year, we are in a pretty safe country. In some regions of the world, the eighth worst danger takes 193 children a day.

Nevertheless, we mustn't get complacent with our safety practices. Biking deaths are not astronomical, but injuries are.

Only one in five children wears a helmet when biking. This is a total disgrace. Parents say they enforce the helmet rule, but they don't. Every bike excursion becomes an exception: "It's only across the street." "It is only down the block." "The other boys aren't wearing helmets." "I don't want to embarrass my child."

Being near to home is the worst excuse, because most accidents happen on secondary roads within a mile of home (but not at intersections).

Many kids don't obey traffic rules, which apply to bikes as well as motor vehicles. Bad bike riding coupled with no helmets is a recipe for disaster. Eighty percent of accidents are the bicyclist's fault, from going too fast, not obeying stop signs, riding into the street without looking or stopping, turning into traffic, or riding against the flow of traffic. Riding against the flow of traffic often feels safer when there are no bike lanes, but a bike is technically a vehicle and must go with the flow of traffic. In some states, you can be ticketed.

Girls on bikes are usually fine about crossing at intersections. Boys, however, usually decide to turn in the middle of the block. They don't look, they turn across traffic without signaling, and they aren't wearing helmets.

Parents don't get tough about making their child wear a helmet. Many think they will turn a boy into a sissy if they make him wear a helmet. This attitude must change.

Reality Check

✓ Bicycle deaths that involve a car collision: 158.

✓ Bicycle deaths that do not involve a car collision: 35.

✓ Three-fourths of bicycle deaths are of boys under age fourteen. White boys are at the greatest risk.

✓ Emergency room treatment for bike-related injuries: 373,000 children, ages five to fourteen.

✓ Scooter accident injuries: 43,900 children under age fourteen.

✓ Most accidents happen from April to October between 2:00 and 8:00 PM.

✓ Children ages ten to fourteen are the least likely to wear helmets.

Preventative Tips

Kids must wear helmets, and so should adults. Bike helmets, like seat belts, are for life.

Teach riding safety and the rules of the road to kids, especially boys. Treat it like on-the-job training for when they get cars.

Parents' Worry Number 9: School Buses

"I never worry about my children riding school buses. It never crosses my mind—because I would never let my child ride a school bus, even if you paid me a million dollars," said a paranoid mom who is a friend of mine. "That's because I drive them myself every single day!"

You know what I am going to say: she is wrong. Driving your child to school is much riskier.

School buses, taking children to and from *school*, have a great safety record. Getting on and off the bus is the risky part, but it's also the part that is under your and your child's control.

Buses have blind spots. Most children are killed or seriously injured by being run over by the bus while they are trying to get on it and are in the driver's blind spot. Even more accidents happen while children are getting off the bus, at about four o'clock in the afternoon. If your children have to get off the bus and then cross the street to walk home, teach them to wait for the bus to leave and show them how to then cross safely.

That's the situation for the trip to and from school. However, many schools also use school buses for field trips to local museums and other sites. For these long-distance journeys, there is no requirement for school authorities to provide safety statistics.

Living for a time in a mountain town in Colorado, a field trip from my kids' school to the museum meant sixty miles down the mountain and sixty miles back up the mountain, often in a blizzard (as it snowed every month except July). I was not comfortable with my children riding on a bus, without seat belts, on icy roads with zero visibility. Since I could not get any information to support the bus safety record, I would not allow my children to go.

Use your common sense to dictate whether you allow your child to travel long distances on a school bus. Think for yourself. Don't assume that it's okay just because the principal says it is okay. You are the parent, and you are in control of your child's activities.

Reality Check

✓ In 2003, twenty children ages fourteen and under were killed in school bus incidents.

✓ Of these twenty deaths, eight (40 percent) were child pedestrians who were struck by buses, not children riding on the buses.

✓ Four of the eight who were killed were between five and seven years old.

✓ Most of these deaths occurred while the children were boarding or exiting the bus and involved the driver's blind spot.

✓ Most pedestrian deaths occur in the afternoon.

✓ In 2003, 6,200 children ages fourteen and under were injured in school bus incidents.

Real Danger Number 9:
Unintentional Poisoning

New parents are oversold kits that enable them to lock up their kitchen cleaners, but they forget the rest of the house. Parents spend hours, days, and years trying to devise safe ways to store turpentine, laundry detergent, and household cleaners, but then they forget to secure art supplies, home repair products, medicine, alcohol, and the big foe—beauty and hygiene products. Something as seemingly innocuous as pink nail polish can be a killer. Drinking perfume and nail polish remover sends 20,000 kids a year to emergency rooms. Toothpaste, hand cream, and hair-care products account for another 13,000 visits. Parents childproof household cleaners but leave anything from laundry detergent to art supplies out for their toddlers.

The preschool years could almost be called the poison control years. One in twenty kids under the age of five goes to the emergency room each year for poisoning—and even more visit doctors' offices. While the parents are trying to find where they put the safety scissors, the little ones are eating glue and crayons.

Childproofing should not be about buying things to lock up dangers. It should be about decluttering and getting rid of dangers. You aren't going to use the old art set. Do you need that old makeup? You will be less stressed if you get rid of 80 percent of your stuff. Then you will know where everything you need is, and you can put all the poisons up high and out of reach until your children are old enough to learn the dangers.

It is up to you to teach them these dangers; no one else will. Don't forget to teach them not to play "survivor" and drink "wee."

Children will put anything in their mouths. Six kids a year go to the hospital for trying to swallow golf balls! These may not be poisonous, but kids will try to put everything in their mouths. Another leading danger is desiccants, those little packets that come in things like vitamin supplements, toys, and electronic products to serve as drying agents. 1.2 million little children are writhing in pain with parents frantic with worry, and these poisonings are all avoidable. Again, that is one in twenty pre-Ks having some poison incident.

Reality Check

✓ Approximately seventy children under age five die from poisonings each year.

Preventative Tips

Stop childproofing your house, or at least rethink your approach. Cabinet locks for toxins aren't the way to go. Child locks only call attention to the locked doors or the Blue Ray disc player. Child locks keep parents out and make life totally inconvenient, but a child can get through one of those locks like an expert safe cracker.

Teach your children that nothing goes in the mouth except food. Nothing!

Parents' Worry Number 10:
Natural Disasters

Parents say that natural disasters are a big worry, and some store food and water and keep portable generators. However, you are more likely to be murdered or die in a household fire.

We can't control the weather, but we are so obsessed by it that we watch the Weather Channel like audiovisual wallpaper during the day.

We won't go to the basement during a tornado warning because it is inconvenient and it scares the kids, but we will jump into the car to "storm chase" a tornado.

The warning systems for natural disasters are really very good. So what should we fear most: tornadoes, hurricanes, earthquakes, avalanches, wildfires, or lightning? None of the above. Flash floods are the biggest killer.

Preventative Tips

Floods. Keeping tools in your car in case you need to break the windshield is a sensible precaution. Rolling down the windows if your car is stuck in rising water should be your first and automatic action. If you can't break the closed windows, you will not be able to open the car door until the car is completely flooded.

Lightning. You really do need to come inside when there is lightning. My kids' tennis lessons were rained out six weeks in a row. The teacher didn't get paid if the lesson didn't go the full hour, so by week four she was saying that it's okay to play tennis during a thunderstorm. It is not. When we lived in London, every summer someone got struck by lightning in our local park. Some died; some survived. Some were playing outside during the thunderstorm. Some took cover and huddled against a tree. Both are wrong actions. Teach your kids that if they can't get out of an exposed area, they should make themselves small by crouching down, but their hands should not touch the ground. Touching a tall tree, standing in the middle of a field, or holding a tennis racket on an exposed tennis court during a lightning storm are not okay.

General disasters. Prepare your family and your home for natural disasters. Have an escape route, extra food, water, copies of insurance documents, flashlights (not candles, which can cause a gas leak to explode), and spare cash.

Remember, severe weather warnings are to be taken seriously.

Real Danger Number 10: Everything Else

Everything you think of could be a danger, so where are you going to draw the line? You really can't fix everything. Your job as a parent cannot be to protect your child from every possibility.

One child nearly suffocated on newspaper. Do you stop reading newspapers? Parents must decide. Are they going to worry about everything? Beyond the top-ten list, there are so many dangers that are equally likely but all are rare.

As many as 10,000 children have strokes each year. Do you

worry about that daily? Maybe you should. When are you going to choose to worry and when are you just going to say, "Enough. I can't worry about everything." Shifting your focus away from worrying about everything is a total change in parenting style.

Chapter Five

Age-Group Essentials: Overview

Sometimes it feels like you are back to square one when your child enters a new phase. You almost need a baby shower for the "new parent of a K–5" or a "new parent of a tween" to get prepared for each stage.

Parents who chorus in unison, "We worry about *everything*" need not just a new parenting ethos, but one for each age group. Getting to the point where you can stand back, watch from a distance, and not speak, nag, or intervene unless death or head injury is imminent takes some serious rethinking about your parenting technique.

Common sense is the cheapest child protection, but it is out of alignment for many of us. In order to protect our children and give them the advantages that we think they need and deserve in the world, we resort to some interesting lion or lioness at-siege parenting.

Let us look at some examples of our past criminal behavior—excuse me, I mean parenting skills:

1. *Felony assault.* We will knock to the ground and trample innocent toddlers to get our child first in the Minnie Mouse autograph line.

2. *Cheating.* We will do almost the entire second-grade science-fair project and pass it off as our darling's own work. (Many schools are stopping science fairs and the like because the entries were actually the "parents' homework." Some poor child whose parents actually made him or her do the project on their own would become completely demoralized, being in direct competition with marketing directors, ad executives, and Fortune 500 presidents.)

3. *Lying.* We will falsify the Girl Scout badge requirements so that our princess doesn't fall behind in the great badge race (we will never find time to sew on the badge, anyway).

4. *Reckless driving.* We will run every stoplight and speed limit to make it to school pickup, and we will even make groups of children scatter and flee to avoid being plowed down by our SUV monster.

5. *Verbal attack on a minor.* We will put down our child's know-it-all friend who deservedly boasts about getting straight A pluses because it makes us and/or our child feel better.

6. *Misleading information.* We exaggerate our brilliant children's achievements to get them in a coveted "gifted and talented" program, college, or "just" the top nursery school.

7. *Theft.* We take both the free cookies and the free apples at Whole Foods in order to appease the kids.

We get overwhelmed. We lose our common sense and decency. We start practicing "over-the-edge" parenting.

Developing a parenting eagle eye on priorities means knowing the facts and statistics, and many Americans don't like numbers. Many of us prefer the drama, the human interest story. Statistics turn us off; human interest turns on our giving feelings. We hate numbers the way we hate snakes and heights. For two-thirds of Americans, "numbers" fall into the "fear and loathing" category. So Americans, by nature, don't go the full way to look at the odds. Don't let a hatred of numbers trick us out of our common sense.

Below are the real statistics about childhood and young adult deaths and the percentages that are due to accidents. (These figures do not include homicide or suicide.) Your natural reflex will be to "knock wood" or cross yourself or "pray God"—but let's be very brave and face our fears head on. And please remember we are looking at over 100 million children and young adults overall.

Reality Check

Under one year old:

✓ Approximately 28,000 deaths a year out of approximately 4.3 million.

✓ 19,000 preterm baby deaths.

✓ From accidents: approximately 1,000.

Ages one to four (of approximately 16 million):

✓ Approximately 4,900 deaths a year

✓ From accidents: approximately 1,600.

Ages five to fourteen (of approximately 40 million):

✓ Approximately 6,900 deaths a year.

✓ From accidents: approx. 2,300.

Ages fifteen to twenty-four (of approximately 42 million):

✓ Approximately 33,000 deaths a year.

✓ From accidents: approximately 16,000

The Preventables: Accidents Are Mostly in Your Control

For each age group, we will provide the number of fatal accidents that are, for the most part, preventable. Freak accidents do happen, and you can't patrol every moment in your children's lives. But drunk driving, for instance, is preventable. Fires and drowning are also largely preventable, as are the others on our list. Some topics overlap into different age groups, but the sections are included in the age group when the topic is most significant or to allow you to take action at the right time to avoid difficulties later.

This discussion won't include cancer, birth defects, pneumonia, and flu. Hard as you may try to sanitize everything, you will undoubtedly miss the one spot your kid touches. All sicknesses are not preventable. Your child will be exposed to illness. As long as you get flu shots and take your sick child to the doctor as appropriate, short of putting your child into a contamination-free room in a biosuit, there is nothing more you can do.

Kids need to get sick to build up immunity. They need to be

exposed to dirt, pollen, and even questionably clean public places.

You can, however, make your kids buckle up. You can avoid that drink before driving the kids. You can keep the pool gate locked. You can put a lock on the gun case and store the ammunition elsewhere. You can take the car keys away if your teen drives six kids in his car.

By personally doing things differently, you have the power to prevent most of the big dangers for your kids.

Chapter Six

Infants

Is a baby registry list of 200 safety products necessary? Does it take two months of research and deliberation to pick the right stroller and baby car seat? With headlines that the U.S. child mortality rate is worse than that of twenty-three other countries, and with 28,000 babies under age one dying every year, new expectant mothers may feel afraid. In 1960, the United States had the twelfth-lowest infant mortality rate, and now it is thirty-fourth. But babies are not at risk the way they used to be. They just seem to be at risk, and new parents feel unprepared to cope. Prematurity and birth defects are the main risk.

Again, the headlines obscure the whole picture. The "small print" reveals that 69 percent of the deaths were preterm babies. In 1960, more babies died per 1,000 than now. Other countries' health care is improving. It is of concern that our ranking is worsening, but the headlines imply a desperate state of affairs. Even though we are now thirty-fourth, this is out of hundreds of countries, and the top fifty all have low mortality rates. Actual health spending per child has decreased in the United States, compared to other countries, and that is a concern. Yet the question is this: is it okay to take statistics out of context in order to give the impression of a far worse situation for the sake of a genuinely needy cause?

Fewer than 950 babies die annually from accidents. Many of these are auto accidents. This leaves a small number out of 4.3 million at "imminent risk," in the words of the baby manufacturing industry.

Large baby chains do a wonderful job of presenting the new parent with everything on the market. It is a free country, and having unlimited free choice is wonderful. But *Consumer Reports* and pediatric authorities have called for a ban on many baby products, ranging from portable baby baths to certain stair gates to some baby bouncers, and more. Some large baby chains we have researched stock so many of these items that more than 30 percent of their products are on a "should-be-banned" list!

The ability to find exactly what you want for your baby is fantastic, but that must be balanced with making the right consumer choices. New moms are almost fanatical about research, so check *Consumer Reports* and the American Academy of Pediatrics' lists about questionable products. This is as important as checking toy recalls.

Some things are essential, like a car seat, a stroller, or a baby carrier, and some are better than others. Door bouncers are "out" for good as highly dangerous in several ways. Pacifiers are "in" to help to prevent crib death. Baby baths are a definite no. But the massive baby-safety market that has taken hold is out of proportion with the actual danger risks. Special blankets, mattresses, toys, and baby-body products are nice to have, but your child will not be permanently disadvantaged by not having a baby computer or a baby-wipe warmer.

Every statistic is a child and therefore a tragedy, which is why there are so many books and magazines devoted to protecting children from every possibility. *The Consumer Reports Guide to Childproofing and Safety: Tips to Protect Your Baby and Child from Injury at Home and on the Go* advises more than 600 things you must do to ensure your baby's safety. Is your child really threatened by 600 imminent dangers that require urgent attention? Are there more, or are there fewer? Six hundred sounds pretty scary to me. I would assume that I'd better run out and buy at least 500 of the fixes immediately (for a baby who can't even walk yet).

Most safety devices are "saving" babies from things that actually are not a danger in the first place. One thousand babies dying from multiple causes is a tragedy. But one thousand out of more than 4.3 million is not an epidemic that requires millions of dollars to be spent on every possible protective device.

Being a paranoid parent myself at one time, I loved our home apnea (breathing) monitor. This was a pad that my daughter slept on (or rolled off of a lot), and it was linked to the intercom I had to listen for her cries. I didn't mind running up and down the stairs continually with every false alarm. The beep-beep made me content. I finally outgrew it. Listening to my child's every breath kept me calm. Did it do anything important as it was not a medical requirement? No, and it seems they have been discontinued as a commercial product.

Parents are so busy fitting electrical outlet protectors and DVD player guards that they forget to secure heavy bookshelves, window blinds, and windows. The problem is often laziness. It is harder to secure a bookcase than an outlet plug, and securing a bookcase can damage the wall. So we think that if we install fifty electrical outlet covers, we have "put in our time" childproofing. We should focus on protection from significant dangers.

Most accidents are usually the fault of parents' not paying enough attention: leaving the baby in the bath to get the door; not buckling the baby in the car seat properly; leaving the baby unstrapped on a changing table; not putting on the stroller parking brake; not having stair gates; or just not watching the baby.

In any given year, there are half a dozen stroller deaths and three or four baby gate failures. All are tragedies of the greatest magnitude, and all lead to product recalls. The U.S. Consumer Product Safety Commission is the place to go for information. The latest high-chair recall involved 1.2 million chairs. That is 1.2 million accidents waiting to happen, but there were actually only twenty-four injuries, and these were minor bruises and a hairline fracture to the arm. That was one of the largest high-chair recalls. Most products are recalled on the suspicion of a danger before there are any injuries.

How panicked should you be if you have sensible precautions in place? There are baby gates that will not work for your home.

You can try out the gate and return it if it isn't working for your house. It is up to you to stop your toddler from pulling the baby over on his or her head by hanging on to the jogging stroller. (Why do you have a jogging stroller, anyway? They aren't safe, according to consumer and official pediatric agencies. Do not let fashion and fitness trump safety.)

Here are the top-five worst things for a baby (in no particular order):

- Baby bath
- Crib bedding
- Bath safety seat
- Jogging stroller
- Baby bouncer and walker

Here are the most essential items:

- Crib with no drop sides
- Properly installed car seat
- Four-wheel stroller
- Hot water controller
- Window locks and restraints to hold heavy
  furniture to the wall
- PVC-, phthalate-, and BPA-free bottles, teethers, and toys
- Fragrance- and color-free soaps, shampoos, and detergents
- All-in-one seasonal sleep sack (no blankets)
- Cloth or disposable diapers, depending on the region.
  (To leave the least carbon footprint: In arid desert climates

with wide open spaces, use disposable diapers; in cities or areas with plentiful water, use cloth diapers.)

After birth-related problems, which are dealt with by medical personnel, the responsibility for a baby's safety is the parents'. Cars and maltreatment are the main dangers.

Navigating the World of Seals of Approval and Consumer Studies and Recommendations

Some consumer manuals on childproofing follow the approach of telling parents how to protect from every possible danger that could befall their children. They do not take into account the likelihood or the seriousness of the danger. It makes the parent who came up with 125 worries in five minutes look like a slacker mom.

These comprehensive guides will give you a fix for every-thing—as many as 200 things you must do for each age group: helmets for learning to walk, special padding so knees aren't bruised, covers for the stove controls. Some even suggest that you should never allow your child into the kitchen until he or she is in kindergarten. (Yeah, that is really going to happen.)

Dire warnings are made in these books. For instance, never allow your child to play with pots or pans, toy utensils, or play knives, because the child might grab a hot pan off the stove or try to play with a real knife.

A new pregnancy manual lists every imaginable danger in

pregnancy. Every drug, every food, every sport is referenced and cross-referenced. Had that book been available when I was pregnant, I would have run to the bookstore to buy it immediately. Tens of thousands of dangers are listed in microscopic type on hundreds of pages, and I could have looked up everything.

Again, I was trying to get a sense of control. I was not content to leave things to Mother Nature, general common sense, or basic health warnings and advice. The pregnancy warnings book had all the right and real credentials, but many credentials are not always what they appear to be. Most "healthy" seals of approval are not what the public perceives them to be.

The Good Housekeeping Seal of Approval, for instance, is simply an extended two-year warranty and not a lab-tested quality product, as it is usually perceived. Quality testing is another aspect of Good Housekeeping, but not the "seal" as you would assume. The participating company promises to replace a product if it goes faulty in two years. That was valuable in the 1960s, but now there are automatic warranties.

Other seals are also not what they seem. Companies that pay to display one healthy seal only have to agree to *try* to make healthier products during the next *twenty* years. Agreeing to try to make a better product in the distant future does not make the product displaying the seal necessarily healthy. We are assuming the seal means a healthy product now. Most "best products" awards and seals are marketing tools set up by advertising companies as a way to drive sales. They appear to be independent awards but are paid for by the manufacturers to an advertising company. The manufacturers pay the advertising company for their product to win the award to drive up their sales volume.

Also beware of the "most popular" award. Consumers who are looking for a product distinction go for the award-winning one, but the award may be totally bogus. The award winner may simply be the product the store got the best discount on and will make the most profit from.

I once overheard a new mom who wanted only the best for her child. She was bouncing her beautiful three-month-old baby girl, who was wearing a designer silver headband, on her lap, and said, "I just had to buy her the Baby Einstein baby bouncer yesterday, but her feet don't reach. [Bouncers are dangerous at this age.] And I am trying *Your Baby Can Read* so she can read at nine months—she will be one of those babies—and *Brainetics,* so she can multiply and get the right answer by kindergarten."

Tension Tamer:

Doing your best for your child doesn't mean buying the most. Doing your best doesn't mean sacrificing yourself. Your children want you more than things.

I am not challenging whether or not certain products work. I am just demonstrating our desperation to want everything for our children. This woman and her husband were taking in boarders so they could afford to buy everything for their tiny baby. How can I tell her that she is probably all wrong in everything she is doing for her most valued "possession," this child whom she loves more than the world? She also mentions kidnapping as her major fear but brings strangers into her home so she can afford new things for the baby.

These are the parents I see everywhere. The best parents in the world will forever be disappointed in their children who are not Einsteins at nine months or nineteen years, because the parents sacrificed everything for that goal. In the process, these parents will create self-entitled, spoiled monsters with low self-esteem who will feel like failures because they didn't read and do calculus by age five.

Chapter Seven

Toddlers

Prekindergarten Years:
I Spy with My Little Eye—My Child

Preschool is the one age when you really *shouldn't* take your eyes off your children. But that doesn't mean around-the-clock surveillance when they are at nursery or day care or when you leave them with the babysitter. Choosing a nursery school that has CCTV cameras and Internet links so that you can watch what your child is doing every second of the day while you are at work is catering to your own guilt and is not helpful to your child.

The argument is made that parents worry less when they are able to tune in to their child. But watching can actually increase parent worry when the caretaker seems to favor another child, your child gets into a disagreement, or your child gets hurt.

Learn how to communicate with your child to find out what he or she is doing in preschool. Talk to his or her teachers instead of confining your knowledge to a highly scrutinized fish bowl.

Controlling and manipulating the teachers, with knowledge of their every movement being scrutinized, is most paranoid parents' goal; but it is not allowing your child to develop properly. Teachers need the freedom to teach, discipline, and regulate your child.

This is also the time when first-time parents, especially, get ahead of themselves, wanting to turn their now-talking little person into a well-rounded, excelling achiever. I bought my two-year-old a complete train set, a bike, and ballet gear for Christmas. What was I thinking? Children don't need a bike at two. Football will wait, as will swim team. George Balanchine, the famous ballet master, said that baby ballerinas should not even "turn out" (the walking-like-a-duck look when ballerinas rotate the legs outward from the hips) until they are at least six years old.

Annual Number of Deaths by Accident and Homicide: Ages One to Four

Motor vehicle	502
Drowning	456
Fire or burn	229
Suffocation	159
Homicide, unspecified	153
Pedestrian	116
Homicide, other, specified	84
Fall	54
Homicide, firearm	54
Poisoning	49

Many parents become obsessed with preparation for nursery school or kindergarten. Don't push. Don't rush. Your toddlers will grow up soon enough. Don't obsess about milestones. Obviously, you should look at developmental milestones occasionally, but remind yourself that pretty much all normal children can talk, write their names, get dressed, and will be potty-trained by the time they leave high school.

Deal with speech and genuine learning difficulties. Don't let academic delay go unchecked, so look for a physical answer if there is a problem. But be aware that some children are more and some are less mature.

Do expose kids to pre-K skills, like numbers, the alphabet, and simple skills like running so they aren't overwhelmed by all they have to learn in kindergarten and will have the self-esteem to tackle new challenges. But don't expect them to fully learn all or any of the skills at this age.

Tension Tamer:

Average children will be able to tie their shoes, use the toilet, write their names, and read by the time they graduate from high school.

Don't compare your child with every child you see. Some children will not be able to coordinate skipping until seven, most can't coordinate swimming the crawl until five, but most will be potty trained before four.

Parental Worry: Is Sugar Making My Child Hyper?

It's a fact: a dealer will peddle a brain-altering, mood-changing, psychologically addicting drug to your three-year-old before your very eyes. This is true. Except for the stranger part. We'll return to the identity of the dealer in a moment.

What drug upsets the chemical balance of the brain? Causes your sweet four-year-old to crave her next high? Results in devastating lows, tears, and tantrums? Suppresses the immune system? Initiates hyperactivity that limits children's ability to concentrate and learn? Reduces the body's ability to fight bacterial infections? Interferes with the absorption of calcium and magnesium? Is transformed into fat more than twice as fast as starch? Has the capability of increasing attention-deficit/hyperactivitiy disorder (ADHD) symptoms? Is fiercely addictive? Inhibits the function of a child's brain synapses?

Yet this drug is considered safe by the overwhelming majority of parents. It's often given as a reward for good behavior, and it's perfectly legal.

If you guessed sugar, you are right. Sugar is not *like* a drug; it *is* a drug. It's the danger that parents are never paranoid enough about.

Reality Check
✓ American kids eat a mind-boggling *3 pounds* of sugar a week; that's more than 150 pounds a year. It's a monumental increase from twenty years ago, when half a pound a week was the norm.

How to Decrease Your Child's Sugar Intake

And kids don't get there by themselves. This drug is given to them by their aunts, their uncles, and their grandparents. Even well-intentioned parents who replace chocolate bars with fruit juice can wind up with drinks that often contain more than double the amount of sugar than candy does.

In our culture, it's virtually impossible to cut out sugar entirely—it's found in processed staples such as bread, sauces, canned goods, frozen foods, and meat products, and it's pushed at theme parks in thirty-two-ounce soft drinks with bottomless free refills.

So what's a parent to do? First, be aware. Second, read the labels on processed foods and juices. For example, many fruit drinks have little real fruit and lots of sugar. Just because a processed food is dubbed "organic" doesn't mean that it doesn't contain a high percentage of sugar. Organic white sugar is still sugar. In fact, sugar of any color is still sugar. Third, stop letting your child sip on soft drinks. Seventy-two percent of children and teens drink more soda than milk.

Stop the soft drink habit. Delay introducing juice for as long as possible. Once you put a juice box in the lunch box, your kids will want that over water. If you must give a sweet treat, first serve a healthy snack of a vegetable, cheese, yogurt, or fruit. Make a rule: No junk without a healthy snack first. Then brush those teeth. (I am never without sugar-free gum.)

Treat sugar like the drug it is. Wean your child off it. For breakfast, don't serve sugary cereals, toaster pastries, and cinnamon rolls. Often they're as full of sugar as a Coca-Cola coupled with a chocolate bar. Replace these high-sugar foods with a low-fat yogurt smoothie or a carbohydrate-protein combination. It may take a couple of extra minutes to blend real fruit, protein, omega supplements, and fiber, but avoiding sugar-related highs and lows could save you a tantrum in the market. For school-age children, the omega supplements appear to boost brain action and calm nerves, and the fiber will fill them and provide calories that will energize them for longer periods. Good-bye, sugar highs and lows. (Reread this paragraph, and tell me you don't feel calmer already.)

When most parents were young, their own parents served dessert and candy as a reward. Break this habit for your own kids. Identify more long-lasting, confidence-building incentives for good behavior: love, praise, time for a cherished activity— whether it's reading or a sport. Parents create a lifelong psychological addiction by rewarding children with sugar in place of love and praise. Not only do the children develop a taste for sugary foods, these foods become associated with love, praise, Mom, and comfort, and the children thus learn to return to these for reward or consolation the rest of their lives.

At tae kwon do, at a school play, and waiting for sis to finish ballet class, moms and dads give in to toddlers by handing over a high-sugar, caffeinated soft drink and a chocolate bar to keep them quiet. That lasts about ten minutes, only as long as they are eating and drinking. In the end, all it serves to do is to unleash a child ten times as noisy and out of control for the next hour. What are parents thinking?

Motivate your children by *being* sweet, not by giving them sweets. While you're at it, see if you can't cut back on sugar a little yourself. There's nothing like a good role model for teaching good habits.

The Age of Poisoning

One in twenty kids under the age of five goes to the emergency room each year for poisoning. Poisoning is a problem with toddlers more than with any other age group. Review the section "Real Danger Number 9: Unintentional Poisoning" (see page 99) for the dos and don'ts on this issue. And remember: teach your kids that nothing goes into the mouth except food.

Here is a list of the number and types of incidents, in an average year, of poisoning of children ages five and under:

Acid
- Acetone, 523
- Hydrochloric acid, 180
- Hydrofluoric acid, 170
- Other, 620
- Unknown, 39

Adhesives, glue, 8,701
Alcohols, 17,026
Ammonia cleaner (all-purpose) 1,501
Animal and insect bites and venom, 15,560
- Ant, 1,105
- Aquatic coelenterate (jellyfish and the like), 151
- Bat, 52
- Bee, wasp, hornet, 2,827
- Black widow spider, 216
- Brown recluse spider, 226
- Cat, 134
- Caterpillar, 705
- Centipede, millipede, 39
- Copperhead snake, 27
- Coral snake, 7
- Cottonmouth snake, 4
- Dog, 378
- Fox, 2
- Mosquito, 133
- Raccoon, 9
- Rattlesnake, 38
- Rodent, 470
- Scorpion, 1,023
- Skunk, 31
- Tarantula, 29
- Tick, 769
- Other insects, 3,408
- Other mammals, 266
- Other reptiles, 397
- Other sea creatures, 321
- Other snakes, 165
- Other spiders, 1,219

Arts, crafts, office supplies, 29,898
- Artist paints, non–water color, 728
- Artist paints, water color, 3,103
- Chalk, 1,762
- Clay, 1,681
- Correction fluid, 1,742
- Crayon, 2,285
- Glaze, 102
- Miscellaneous, 182
- Pencil, 1,866
- Pen, ink, 10,768
- Other, 5,378
- Unknown, 301

Ashes, 530
Automotive, aircraft, boat products, 4,478
Ashes, 530
Automotive, aircraft, boat products, 4,478

Batteries, 3,771
Bleach
•Borate, 238
•Hypochlorite, 21,461
•Nonhypochlorite, 527
•Other, 110
Bubble-blowing solutions, 4,332
Building and construction products, 5,659
Carpet and upholstery cleaner, 3,740
Charcoal, 737
Chemicals, 15,766
•Alkali, 1,179
•Ammonia, 1,374
•Borates, boric acid, 1,817
•Chlorates, 13
•Cyanide, 13
•Dioxin, 2
•Formaldehyde, formalin, 201
•Glycol, ethylene, 151
•Glycol, other, 595
•Ketones, 253
•Methylene chloride, 100
•Nitrates, nitrites, 275
•Phenol, creosote, 225
•Strychnine, 27
•Toluene diisocyanate, 105
•Other, 6,384
•Unknown, 1,520
Christmas ornaments, 989
Cleansers
•Anionic, nonionic, 2,876
•Other, 806
Coins, 2,879
Combustibles, 1,950
•Explosives, 152
•Fireworks, 349
•Matches, 1,421
•Other, 25
•Unknown, 3
Cosmetics, personal care products, 157,550
•Bath oil, bubble bath, 8,478
•Cream, lotion, foundation makeup, 15,524

•Dental care products, other, 938
•Deodorants, 9,202
•Depilatories, 328
•Douches, 137
•Eye products, 1,165
•False-teeth cleaning, 280
•Hair-care products, other, 2,339
•Hair-coloring agents, 850
•Hair rinses, conditioners, relaxers, 3,070
•Hairspray, 2,245
•Lipsticks, balms, with camphor, 726
•Lipsticks, balms, without camphor, 2,335
•Mouthwash, ethanol, 3,935
•Mouthwash, fluoride, 1,383
•Mouthwash, nonethanol, 147
•Nail polish, 9,224
•Nail polish remover, acetone, 2,834
•Nail polish remover, other, 1,939
•Nail polish remover, unknown, 7,818
•Perfume, cologne, aftershave, 22,897
•Peroxide, 7,498
•Powder, talc, 4,170
•Powder, nontalc, 1,305
•Shampoo, 7,015
•Soap, 12,266
•Suntan, sunscreen, 6,350
•Toothpaste, fluoride, 17,865
•Toothpaste, nonfluoride, 572
Deodorizers, 15,467
•Air fresheners, 11,620
•Diaper pail deodorizers, 347
•Toilet bowl deodorizers, 812
•Other, 2,630
•Unknown, 58
Desiccants, 27,647
Disinfectant
•Hypochlorite, 5,270
•Phenol, 2,556
•Pine oil, 7,030
•Other, 1,760
Dishwashing detergent, automatic
•Granules, 5,134
•Liquid, 2,582

•Rinse agents, 1,243
•Other, 822
•Unknown, 821
Dishwashing detergent, hand
•Anionic, nonionic, 5,543
•Other, 699
Drain cleaner
•Acid, 92
•Alkali, 668
•Other, 84
Dye, 2,178
•Food coloring (e.g., Easter egg), 879
•Leather, 98
•Other, 454
•Unknown, 35
Essential oils, 2,785
Fabric softener, antistatic agents
•Aerosol spray, 21
•Dry powder, 2
•Liquid, 1,101
•Solid sheet, 312
•Other, 37
Feces, urine, 4,242
Fertilizer, lawn and household plant, 7,377
Fire extinguisher, 284
Food products, food poisoning, 22,469
•Mushrooms, 6,796
Glass, 765
Glass cleaner
•Ammonia, 1,610
•Anionic, nonionic, 31
•Isopropanol, 5,573
•Other, 3,008
Hydrocarbons (gasoline, lighter fluid, mineral spirits), 26,018
Incense, 245
Lacrimators (e.g., tear gas), 1,100
Laundry additives
•Bluing, brightening agent, 41
•Detergent booster, 25
•Enzyme, microbiological additive, 69
•Water softener, 15

•Other, 458
Laundry detergent
•Granules, 6,403
•Liquid, 2,510
•Soap, 103
•Other, 80
Laundry prewash, stain remover
•Dry solvent-based, 102
•Liquid solvent-based, 333
•Spray solvent-based, 346
•Other solvent-based, 26
•Dry surfactant-based, 257
•Liquid surfactant-based, 1,752
•Spray surfactant-based, 243
•Other surfactant-based, 16
•Other, 26
Miscellaneous substances, 5,764
Oven cleaner
•Acid, 16
•Alkali, 917
•Detergent, 8
•Other, 59
Paint, stripping agents, 13,571
Photographic products, 276
Plants, 84,185
Polish, wax, 5,901
Radioisotopes, 15
Repellent, pesticide, 28,839
•Insect, 4,942
•Moth, 3,528
•Rodent, 17,608
Rust remover
•Alkali, 7
•Hydrofluoric acid, 96
•Other acid, 255
Soil, 2,103
Sporting equipment, 478
•Golf balls, 7
Swimming pool, aquarium, 3,567
Thermometer, 8,414
Tobacco products, 7,923
Toys, 5,942
Total nonpharmaceutical substances, 731,407

This list, believe it or not, represents only *half* of what kids are getting into! It does not include pharmaceutical products.

These poisonings are almost all 100 percent preventable. Keeping your eyes on your kids 24/7 won't last forever, but it's important at this age. And you will be begging to go to kindergarten with them to keep your eyes on them. So don't slack off when it counts. Parenting vigilance is hard work—but that should be in the parent job description.

Preventative Tips

Don't overdo the purchase of childproofing gadgets. Give away clutter, and don't buy more. It is a clutter-control issue. Recycle old ink cartridges. Find an alternative for mothballs. Throw away old packaging. Put personal hygiene products up high. Arts and crafts are not babysitters while you take a shower. Crawl around on the floor and pick up everything. Again, above all, teach that nothing goes in your mouth except food.

Parental Worry: Germy Shopping Carts or Avoiding the Spill in Aisle Three

Do you go into defense mode when you leave the house? Normally, I would say that the outside world is safer than home, but there is one exception. Do you know what can be a dangerous locale if you don't plan correctly?

The grocery store. Yes, the one that's only five minutes from your house. It's true—and it's all in the shopping cart.

Shopping cart–related accidents account for a nerve-wracking 35,000 trips to hospital emergency rooms for children under the age of fourteen.

You are thinking germs. You grab the disinfectant wipe or your own sanitizer and scrub down the cart. You buy beautiful cloth baby-seat protectors that you dutifully wash for shopping trips. Once the cart is sanitized, you let the older kids "help with the shopping" by letting them push the younger sibling in the cart. Or you are letting the older kids ride in the cart like it's a theme park ride, to keep them occupied while you see to the shopping.

You are thinking head cold; we are thinking head injury. What we are dealing with is the most badly designed baby and child hazard around: the shopping cart. Shopping carts are so dangerous that the U.S. Consumer Product Safety Commission wants them banned until they are redesigned. Why? They are a leading cause of serious brain trauma. Permanent brain injury is one of doctors' biggest fears and needs to become a legitimate concern for parents.

A full 74 percent of shopping cart accidents result in neck or head injuries for the children involved. According to the Department of Pediatrics at the Ohio State University College of Medicine and Public Health, 20,700 children who visit hospital emergency departments for such incidents are under the age of five.

Falling from seven feet onto solid concrete is not lethal, but it is life destroying. Your child probably won't die, but he or she could become a vegetable. (Tact has no place here.)

The good news is that shopping cart injuries are easily preventable.

With a set of triplets, I certainly understand the desperation of any parent attempting to keep children happy on a grocery foray. But it isn't okay for three children of any age to ride in one of those small two-basket carts. It isn't okay for your seven-year-old to use one as a skateboard. It isn't okay to put four-year-old twins on the top of a kiddie-car shopping cart and leave them to fight standing up. And it isn't okay that a five-year-old pushes a baby in an unfixed car seat that is balanced on the top of the cart.

According to the American Academy of Pediatrics, the best solution is this: Don't put your child in a cart at all. Bring another adult to care for him or her, have an older child walk with the younger child, or leave your children at home with another adult. (I know, these just aren't always real-world possibilities.)

In terms of my life, the above options are dreams. So here are the essentials for keeping your child safe while in a shopping cart. Always place a child in a safety belt or a harness. Straps are good, but they're useless if your hyper five-year-old flips the cart with your infant in it. Never leave a child alone in a cart. Teach your children that shopping carts are not toys or rides. They'll appreciate the responsibility. Don't let them stand or move around in them, and *never* let them ride on the outside of them. If you have a choice, all kids should stay out of the cart!

Baskets are for groceries, not kids. Follow these steps as you shop, and you'll be keeping your child safe.

Preventative Tips

If you must put your child in a shopping cart, use the safety harness. Don't leave your child unattended. Don't let older children touch the cart. A shopping cart is not a ride! Ban the practice of putting children in shopping carts.

Parental Worry: Swimming with Sharks or the Killer on the Beach

Have you ever wondered why paranoia can't take a vacation when you do? Why doesn't it check into a hotel on Oahu while your kids snorkel safely off Maui? Paranoid parents everywhere know how you feel. Why is it that both everyday and international paranoias always sneak into the luggage?

Some parents I have met don't even go on vacations because their worries overwhelm them. They won't go to theme parks. Camping is out until the kids are older. And the thought of the nearby beach has one parent ready to move to the mountains.

Recently a friend told me just such a story. She was lying on a beautiful beach off the coast of Mexico, the weather was outstanding, her husband was out surfing, and her three kids hadn't squabbled for days. She should have been perfectly happy. Instead, she was gripped by terror that her oldest boy, who insisted on snorkeling—which was why they'd come—would be eaten by sharks.

Memories of a young shark-ravaged female athlete recovering to win the Special Olympics will forever be etched on the paranoid mom's brain. We are all carrying around news story memories that are stronger than the memories of the highlights of our own lives.

"Great vacation this is turning out to be," her husband pointed out to her when she shared her fears for the eighty-third time.

I wish she'd called me. What would you guess is the number of shark-attack deaths per year? The answer: one or two. You didn't misread it. Only about fifty shark attacks occur annually, with only one or two fatalities. That's worldwide.

Now envision the number of oceans, countries, and beaches in the world and the number of kayakers, surfers, swimmers, and waders who are out in the water at any given time. You're certainly free to worry, if you like, but the shark scenario is not something I'm going to worry about while I'm waiting for the airline to find my lost luggage.

We don't slack off with our intense worry over sharks, but we often deliberately slack off over the real killer at the beach. The sun. More than half of all sun exposure may happen before the age of fifteen. Too much sun exposure means cancer. One in five people gets skin cancer, and it does kill. It is one of the leading causes of cancer in young people, and most are girls. "Jaws" isn't stalking; the sun is. The solution is a lot easier than what most parents are doing.

Many a paranoid parent's solution is two-hourly applications of two varieties of sunscreen. Sunscreen that's rubbed on a three-year-old, however, always ends up in the eyes, because of all the struggle involved with an uncooperative child. Also, sunscreen manufacturers determine the sun protection (SPF) factor by testing the sunscreen under *indoor* light so its viability is easily questionable.

The simple solution is so much easier, but it requires a change in mindset for most Americans.

Dr. Ned Calonge, the chief medical officer of Colorado, told me about the dilemma that all the heads of state medical departments discuss when they meet. "Sunscreen doesn't work. It doesn't stop most cancers or aging," he said. It does stop sunburn, and bad sunburns can lead to certain cancers. But the majority of the damage is happening anyway.

That sounded like a national news story that no one has heard about. Dr. Calonge said that the health departments are not publicizing it. The health experts don't want to start a panic. Some sunscreen is better than none. We don't want people to give up on letting their kids running around shirtless or bikini-clad all summer. There is an answer, but the health experts think that Americans won't go along with it.

Other sunny countries get it. You need to wear clothes to stop serious sun damage. Australians cover up; so do Indians, Arabs, and Europeans. Americans, however, feel invincible.

This doesn't mean that we have to run out and buy special ultraviolet (UV)-protective clothing. Scott Katzskee, a leading international clothing manufacturer, admitted to me that the sale of UV-protective clothing was down. He thought there were two reasons: the economy—why pay thirty-six dollars for an organic UV-protective T-shirt when you can get an ordinary one for two dollars; and *all* clothing is UV protective unless it gets wet.

UV-protective swimsuits are the best investment, especially if you and your child are in the sun for a long time. But sun damage isn't limited to the beach or pool. Throw on some clothes, a hat, and sunglasses this summer and all year round.

If your toddler lasts about twenty minutes in the pool splashing about in an expensive UV-protective suit but spends the rest of the summer running about shirtless or in a sleeveless sun top, that isn't spending your money sensibly.

Wearing clothes is so much easier than applying and reapplying sunscreen to squirmy kids every two hours. So the new solution is so much easier than the sunscreen squirm and struggle. And it is a simple concept for kids: cover up.

I think the clothes solution is doable for our toddlers, but I don't have great confidence in the success of it with our older daughters. Just try to get your daughter to wear something other than a bikini! Let a doctor talk her through the "freezing off" of precancerous skin growths. That might do it; but remember, the consequences can be even worse.

Preventative Tips

Sunscreen stops sunburn but not the worst cancer-causing skin damage. Only clothes stop cancer-causing skin damage. Make sure that your child is wearing a long-sleeved shirt, a hat, and sunglasses.

Parental Worry: Toy Recalls

Made in China—scary! Plastic toys—never! Wooden toys—yes! Natural toys like pots and pans—yes! Wrong, wrong, wrong!

China was framed. Chinese workers will make toys exactly the way that the manufacturers tell them to make them. The Chinese are highly intelligent and have highly sophisticated manufacturing techniques for making toys for large U.S. manufacturers.

This is big business, with sophisticated product control. But there are always the ruthless manufacturers who will cut corners and put melamine in baby formula or dog food. Contaminated products are the result of deliberate acts, not carelessness or accidents.

Mattel and other U.S. manufacturers tell the Chinese the exact formulas and plans for making and manufacturing their toys and other products. If there was lead in the plastic toys, it was because the U.S. manufacturer approved of that level of lead. This is according to Wendy Bassy, a Paranoid Parents expert consultant. Bassy is a toy manufacturer who deals with China, but she also works with Chinese consumer agencies to study the problems.

Mattel was allowing those lead levels or looking the other way. It was Mattel's fault, but China was blamed. Playing on xenophobic stereotypes, the companies convinced U.S. parents that China was at fault. But "Made in China" is not always bad.

The incorrect strategy of convicting someone without a trial ruined Chinese industry. Many wonderful factories closed, never to reopen. The Mattel confession of guilt came too late to save the Chinese toy industry. Product costs went up, so many U.S. companies could no longer afford to be in business.

Another myth concerns wooden toys. All wood is not equal. Some wood that is used to make wooden toys is soaked in formaldehyde. You don't want your child sucking on this any more than you want your child sucking on plastic.

What makes a toy dangerous is simple: trying to eat it, lick it, or chew on it.

Chewing on plastic or anything containing lead is not okay. In three hours of chewing, your child will absorb higher levels of the substance than the FDA approves for an entire lifetime. Two of the greatest dangers come from your child putting things in his or her mouth: choking and ingesting poisonous chemicals.

Parents must teach their children that nothing goes into the mouth but food (or medicine from the parent or a doctor). *Nothing*, other than food.

Have you ever considered abandoning all toys and having your children use their imaginations by playing in cardboard boxes and using pots and pans? According to *The Consumer Reports Guide to Childproofing and Safety: Tips to Protect Your Baby and Child from Injury at Home and on the Go,* if your children play with real pots and pans, they are more likely to reach up and grab them off the stove and be seriously burned.

I would almost go so far as to say that anything and everything can be dangerous in the hands or the mouth of an unsupervised toddler, but anything is safe when the toddler is supervised.

We worry a lot about toys. Every toy recall sends us rushing—dare I say, panicking—from the computer or television set to the toy box. But the numbers, once again, probably are not what we expect. Between eight and thirteen children under age fifteen die each year from toys. The number varies each year, but the average is about ten children a year out of more than 60 million children. Just a little more than 1 in 10 million is not a nationwide epidemic.

Several categories of dangers exist: young children playing with toys that are suitable only for older children, toys with small or easily breakable parts, and toys that contain dangerous chemicals, lead, and kinds of plastic.

Many toys made with illegal products are still being sold, in spite of legislation and tough requirements. Lead is still found in many toys, and other illegal substances are still present in unregulated toys worldwide. Little girls' jewelry from unknown sources is a particular product that is best avoided. (Chewing on toy jewelry is certainly to be avoided.)

Little girls' makeup is another problem. Any perfume or coloring can be extremely irritating to children. Buy with extreme care. Children can develop allergies even to expensive makeup if it is worn repeatedly. Go fragrance free, too. Never allow children to share their makeup sets.

Balloons are still one of the most dangerous toys, although awareness of this danger has reduced deaths and injuries significantly in recent years. The little pieces of popped balloons can get into the lungs and cause suffocation. If you must buy balloons, buy Mylar. However, protection agencies advise that you don't give your children balloons until they are eight years old. Now you are aware, so you can be vigilant.

Magnetic balls and other small magnets are potentially lethal. If they are accidentally swallowed, they will magnetically connect together in the stomach and the intestines and cause death. Although a potential problem, very few children have been hurt from magnets, especially compared to balloon injuries and deaths.

Reality Check

✓ About 50,000, children age four and under are injured from toys each year.

✓ About 100,000 children ages five to fourteen are injured from toys each year.

✓ Of deaths from toys, 54 percent are from choking, and 43 percent of these were with balloons. This phenomenon is easily prevented.

✓ About 71,500 children were seen in emergency rooms from riding-toy injuries, and 75 percent of these were from motorized vehicles. This phenomenon is easily prevented.

Preventative Tips

Keep everything that is not food or a pacifier out of your children's mouths. Stop them from chewing on whatever they are chewing on. Avoid riding toys. (Mini-Mustangs and Barbie Jeeps cause serious, permanent injuries.)

Parents still panic too much over recalls, but these same parents allow young children to play with toys that are designed for the kids' older siblings. Such toys often have small, swallowable parts. Parents should make sure that they observe age guidelines when they buy toys for their children.

Keeping your eye on your child is still the best safety measure for total toy safety.

Balloon pieces are still a big danger.

Really watch what kind of plastic the toys are made of.

Child-age warning labels are put on toys for a reason.

For Christmas, get plastic ornaments and give age-appropriate toys. The Christmas tree should not be a no-go area for the children. Decorating should be a family activity. The valuable antique, handed-down ornaments can come out in a few years, when the kids are older. Don't worry about offending a relative who buys an inappropriate toy for your child. Make it quietly disappear.

Chapter Eight

Elementary School

Parents of older children will tell you, "It doesn't get any easier." Sometimes they'll even say, "It gets harder the older they get." So is there an age when you can worry less? Actually, there is: between the ages of five and nine. Elementary school children have fewer fatalities overall than the pre-Ks. The time of home poisonings is mostly over. Most accidents now involve cars or from learning new sports.

Especially at this age, because so many child deaths and injuries in the United States are avoidable by taking simple precautions, worrying should be replaced by action. Wear that seat belt, helmet, or sports equipment; follow the rules; stick with a buddy. This is the age when kids will still listen to you when you ask them to put on a helmet or wear a seat belt. Don't scare your children. You are in control, and they will learn to be in control.

If you know that something is dangerous, take control. Do so even if it means standing up to school administrators, coaches, or other parents who don't believe in seat belts or don't lock up their guns. You

Annual Number of Deaths by Accident and Homicide: Ages Five to Nine

Motor vehicle	515
Drowning	142
Fire or burn	118
Homicide, firearm	62
Other land transport	50
Suffocation	37
Homicide, unspecified	24
Pedestrian	22
Nonland transport	21
Poisoning	21
Natural or environmental	17
Death-related injury (out of 20 million kids)	1,275

there are 1,782,568 non-lethal injuries that take kids 5–9 to the ER

know what is dangerous. Teach your children early in life what isn't a good choice, and then keep reminding them. However, you *must* take control in the early years if you want to stop something really serious in the later years. This is your "calm" period, before the storm of the tween years and the hurricane of the teen years.

Tweens and teens are away from the supervising parent and on their own. But elementary-age kids will follow rules and won't question you at every step. As always, car accidents are the major serious threat, but those can be prevented by being buckled in properly. Most of the other injuries are from sports, and these accidents are often the parents' fault for not making sure that the kids are wearing the right gear and following the rules. Most sports accidents happen while learning a sport, especially in the first week. Most accidents happen at practices, not at games, because the practices aren't usually as well supervised, and many practices continue past the children's endurance and attention span.

Why Do We Worry About Our Elementary-Age Kids If They Are Safe?

As I said, parents of young kids often hear the parents of older kids say that they worry about their children more now that they're older than they did when the kids were young. When I was the parent of two-year-old triplets, I thought that those parents were losing their minds or were just slackers.

As children get older the types of worries shift. We are no longer trying to save our child from physical injury as you need to with very small children. Now our children are going out into the real world. Now the dangers are of the heart and the mind: relationships, socialization, being integrated and independent at the same time. Our children are facing the work ethic and moral ethics for the first time.

The toddler lived in his or her own world. *Self* was all important. Now the concept of *self* depends on a bigger circle. Self-esteem, self control, self-motivation, and selflessness are a hard shift from a world of selfishness.

These issues become the parents' new worries. Coping with the outside world, learning to negotiate with other people while staying true to yourself or while finding yourself, is fraught with as many disasters and setbacks as learning to walk.

When your child skins a knee, it is easy to put a bandage on it and get a smile in return. When your child's best friend betrays him or her, there are no easy fixes. Your heart breaks as much as your child's heart does.

Parental Worry: Sports Injuries and Mistakes

This is not a touchy-feely section about easing the agony of defeat. It's about the things parents do that make their kids perform less well at sports and that may even injure the child on a short- or long-term basis.

Sports are great. We want our kids to play sports to learn teamwork and the discipline of practice, because we loved sports, and so that they will be healthy, learn sportsmanship, and won't have time to get in with the "bad" crowd. Along with having all the right reasons, sometimes we think that our talented little Venus Williams might just go pro, with a little proper coaching.

But the statistics tell us that our aspirations for our child going pro should be classed as certifiably insane. Of 10 million white high school basketball players, only twenty-eight will go pro. The odds aren't so much better if you are black: only sixty-five out of 10 million. It's better than the odds of winning the lottery, but not worth sacrificing your child's studies for eight hours of practice a day. Professional football takes 17 kids per 1 million, and baseball takes 14 per 1 million, on the average. But most pro careers last only one season. The management is just trying out the talent—then it's good-bye. For professional golf, you're twice as likely to win the lottery as to become a Tiger Woods. Nevertheless, we still think that our children can do it, if they really try, and even more deluded parents believe that their children really *will* do it. Children see sports people being turned into the nation's heroes, and they start wanting a piece of that misguided dream.

Reality Check

✓ We think that all that work playing sports since elementary school will guarantee a sports scholarship as our child's ticket to college. The reality is that most college kids on a sports scholarship have "injured out" of their sports scholarship before their junior year—so you better not have counted on that money.

How You Help Your Child to Lose at Sports

In fact, most of the things we do to make our child succeed at sports are exactly the *wrong* things. Four things come to mind.

First, we start kids too early. Most kids' bodies and brains are not ready to engage in a serious sport until they are eleven to thirteen. Many kids can't coordinate skipping until they are seven, bike riding alludes many six-year-olds.

I have found parents who pay $150 an hour for their three-year-old to play soccer. I have seen thirteen-year-olds with tennis talent injured for life after years of homeschooling and expensive tennis coaches. One dad hired Prince Harry's British soccer coach for his four-year-old (who was of small stature) so that the boy would have an advantage over his toddler-age soccer friends.

Don't get me wrong. It is extremely important to work on physical skills with our kids at an early age. We need to teach them to kick, throw, skip, jump, run, and ride a bike. The research evidence shows that the more confidence they have as they enter kindergarten, the better they will do in school. But be aware that some kids won't develop this way until later.

Second, because Mom and Dad were great at a particular sport, they expect that little Henry or Jane will have the exact same physique as star-high-school-athlete Mom or Dad and succeed like they did. Your child may have a different body type and will never be good at the parent's sport.

There are three common body types: tall and thin, short and stocky, and average. Tall, lanky kids typically develop late, so they will typically be bad at sports skills until they are seven or older. But these late bloomers usually have more skill than earlier developers because their brains are more developed when they master the skill. Don't expect tall and lanky children to do well at wrestling or short and stocky kids to do well at basketball. The stocky kid who wants to be an athlete could do well at rugby, wrestling, and football, whereas a child with short or normal muscle length might be better suited for running and swimming.

If your child isn't built like you, don't expect him or her to have the success you had in your sport. It isn't about brains and genius timing. The body type has to be right, foremost.

Third, thinking about sports success as a free-ride ticket to a college scholarship is wrong. Sports should be for fun and all those great things you learn. You can enjoy a game without winning. Few athletes will be ultimate winners, the sort that kids see on TV. Academic scholarships are easier to get and are lasting. Coming to college on a sports scholarship, the kid drops a trunk on his or her foot moving into the dorm at the beginning of freshman year and is injured and moves out before classes start. By junior year, most kids on sports scholarships can no longer meet the requirements for their sports scholarship because of injury or the need to concentrate more on their academics.

Fourth, the game is on, and the yelling starts. Stop yelling at your child. Since he or she is unlikely to go pro, it is not worth undermining your relationship. And yelling activates the freeze or flight instinct, so this behavior on your part will probably lead your child to stop altogether or run the wrong way.

Parents often yell their kids into a reptilian brain freeze when they are coaching them. I have heard, "But I yelled at them last week when they messed up, and they did great this week." Don't assume that it was your yelling that improved your child's performance. Your child has a basic skill level; on some days he or she will do better, and on other days he or she will do worse. Being positive will work better in the long run for overall improvement.

Parents are making all these mistakes simultaneously. I met a six-year-old who was tall and lanky and looked older than he was. He was doing three sports, each several times a week: wrestling (wrong body type); ice hockey (his dad had done it); and football (he looked old enough to be ready). None of these sports was necessarily the best sport for a tall kid who, sportswise, would develop late. He might look older, but he didn't have the maturity to play or the maturity to cope with failure. The more he failed, the more sports his dad wanted him to do, and the more anxious and angry his dad became. Consider the money spent: even recreational sports, every day of the week plus games, could run $4,000 a year or more for a six-year-old child. Maybe that money would have been better spent for a little counseling for his pushy dad.

Preventative Tips

Try out different sports. Limit sports to one or two per school term, and make the second one swimming, which is a necessary life skill. If you want to encourage your child to specialize in one sport, wait until he or she is eleven to thirteen. Your goal should be for your child to grow up to do what he or she loves, and that doesn't necessarily include being a world champion. (Yes, for those who still have their eye on the gold medal or Wimbledon trophy or just the sports scholarship, your child can take up a sport at twelve and still become a world champ. Their wide range of skills and their body strength and coordination will be an asset.)

Finding the Right Sport for the Paranoid Parent's Child

Elementary school is when sports injuries start, so prepare for some trips to the emergency room. That can be hard for a paranoid parent to accept. What can the worried parent do to cope? Recognize that some sports are more dangerous than others.

Ice skating is more dangerous than in-line skating. Gymnastics sends a high number of children to the emergency room for minor injuries, but these little injuries translate into the most chronic injuries as adults. The odds are fifty-fifty that your recreational gymnast will end up in the ER this year.

The CDC calls baseball the most lethal popular sport (*lethal* does mean "deadly," but the actual number of deaths is quite low). Note that the CDC's category here is *popular* sports; however, less popular sports can be just as lethal. The most baseball deaths (under a dozen) come from balls hitting heads, not from bat injuries. Baseball is targeted because of the chronic disabilities that appear later in life. "Little league elbow" is as real for ten-year-olds as "tennis elbow" is for three-year-olds put in training by the pushy parents.

More children are hurt cheerleading than playing ice hockey. In sports like gymnastics and, to a lesser degree, cheerleading, approximately 50 percent of participants end up in the emergency room in any given year.

Again, it just isn't what most of us have been led to think. We look at brave little ice hockey players skating like rockets as playing a violent sport. But young ice hockey skaters stop and turn in a safer way than figure skaters do. Figure skaters are setting themselves up for chronic health problems. Injuries from figure skating that seem minor worsen in adulthood.

Ice skaters have more serious head injuries than in-line skaters, roller skaters, and ice hockey skaters. One reason is that ice skaters actually fall differently than "land" skaters. The other reason is that "land" skaters and hockey players wear helmets more consistently than ice skaters do.

Children who want a competitive hobby or a career in skating should skate for safety first, adhering to no triple jumps until after puberty. Triple jumps cause extreme wear and tear on the ankles, the knees, and the hips. Girls should not overstretch during a growth spurt; the bones and the muscles won't grow properly. This applies to any sport.

Preventative Tips

Most accidents happen when children are learning a new sport, so this is when you need to be at each practice. This is far more important than being at each and every game. It might surprise you to learn that most injuries do not happen at games. Games are well supervised, the regulations are maintained, and all the right equipment is worn. All these things may be slack at practices, where there can be a lot of messing around. Lack of skill causes injuries, so work with your child to perfect the skills. And insist that he or she wears the appropriate safety equipment. Safety equipment works fantastically well if your child wears it.

Paranoid parents usually aren't the kind of parents who have

Olympic dreams, so they are unconsciously more likely to want their child to play a sport for life. Encourage sports that your child can play in college recreationally and in adulthood. Golf, tennis, martial arts, running, swimming, skiing, and Frisbee are individual sports that can be played on teams and continued into adulthood. You don't actually find many adults playing soccer, football, or baseball at thirty, no matter how great these are as youth sports.

Parental Worry: Is My Child at the Right School?

Parents are worried hearing rumors that America's schools are failing. The United States ranks number thirty-seven in education, far down the list of the world's countries. Oprah says the ranking is twenty-fourth, but it doesn't really matter since the United States is so far down the chart. If your football team was ranked twenty-fourth or thirty-seventh, you might consider changing teams. How can we prepare our young children to compete in the global job market if standards don't improve? Parents aren't just asking if their child is in the right school, but the right country. Parents have asked me if it is time to move, and by that they mean leave the country, abandon the sinking ship. Let's all move to a different country to educate our kids— pretty much anywhere else in the industrialized world would be better than here.

Parents hear the statistics and think all schools are failing us, from elementary school on up. We need to rethink our entire view of the education rankings at all levels to get our elementary school child's education career on the right course.

When it comes to elementary-school education, the United States is actually doing well in a worldwide context; it *seems* that the older grades are a problem. What happens in older grades that causes such a drastic drop in standards? What can the statistics tell us?

In middle-school education, America ranks fifteenth in the world; high-school education could be as bad as thirty-seventh.

So what happens in middle school and high school? Are all the good teachers in elementary school? Do we have a nation of lazy tweens and teens?

We have great teachers on all levels. The ranking is not a reflection of what happens in our schools, it is a reflection of how other nations calculate their statistics. Other countries start "streaming" children in the middle school years. Some children are categorized as "worthy" of pursuing an academic career, and the others are channeled into trades. Those channeled into trades are no longer counted in the educational achievement rankings.

In the United States, we believe that all children are entitled to a college-prep education, whether or not they are academically inclined. So our ranking reflects every child in the nation, whereas most other countries' rankings reflect the achievements only of those who have been preselected for their academic ability. Comparing U.S. statistics with other countries' statistics is therefore like trying to compare apples with oranges.

As parents and Americans, we believe that every child should go to college. But not all children will be straight-A students. We believe that everyone deserves a chance at a good education. Sometimes our sense of inclusiveness is just a wonderful dream with sad consequences. The seeds are planted in elementary school. But America's approach is to educate all so we count all in our statistics. In other countries, only the smartest are counted.

Some elementary schools are failing our children. Schools in poor areas do not have the same resources as schools in affluent communities. The poor communities, kids, and schools need our support. All elementary school children deserve a great education to prepare them for a life of learning.

Entitlement to a good education and the definition of excellence can be controversial. In England after World War II, a good education was offered to more children, and more children were therefore getting high national test scores. The responses were mixed. Some worried that the tests had been "dumbed down." Others wanted the tests made harder so that academic excellence would be preserved for the very few. Others believed that the results were an achievement of the educational efforts. The U.S. dream of a good education for all is braver than we realize.

We look at our child starting school and feel traumatized that we will create a high-school dropout. This is a phobia many parents of elementary school children carry with them daily. So what is the high-school dropout rate? I would have guessed 30 percent. But no, in this most wonderful state of Colorado, with its low obesity rate, with its cities ranked in the top twenty safest cities, the high-school dropout rate is 50 percent. In a state that gets a lot right, we are getting our most basic necessity—a smart workforce—wrong. These real figures give us new parents of school-age children terrors. Again, these statistics don't tell the whole story. Many of these kids go on to finish, many go to community college, and many enter the workforce where they get more training.

But if we want to get our children on the right path to a good education, we might take an example from abroad. A top London school accepts a diverse set of children, from poverty-line, single-parent families to families with two nannies and a housekeeper. It is an example school of the nation. It is interesting to note that the children from the poor families were never found in the after-school sports or art programs. The children from the poorer families were the ones with computers. Their parents saw education as the ticket to a better life.

So your academic cause is "let us be vigilant":

How can parents be sure that they are sending their children to a good elementary school? When academic funding goes to sniper proofing a school, there will be an educational consequence. Our educational cause should be to improve failing schools and advocate a core education: the three Rs—reading, (w)riting, and 'rithmatic—and science. Ignore national ranking numbers, they don't tell the whole story.

At home, read with your child every day for twenty minutes. If you miss too many of these reading sessions with your child, he or she will fall behind the children who *are* reading daily. Twenty minutes a day, six days a week is two hours a week. That means that in a year, you'll have spent 100 hours reading with or to your children. The benefits of this for you child cannot be overstated. Skip three days a week and your child has only read 50 hours that year. Your child will be way behind the other children.

Parental Worry: Playground Injuries

A dad brought his one-and-a half year old son to the deserted school playground. He meticulously brought out a bike helmet from his big gym bag and strapped it on the little boy. The little boy had a hard enough time walking without a big helmet on, but with it, he staggered left and right just like he was on a ship in a rough sea. The dad then pulled a basketball out of the sports bag, gave his son a gentle push in the direction of the playground equipment, which was suited to second grade and up, and the dad headed for the nearby court area to shoot a few hoops.

The little boy made it to the top of the play set and was walking straight off the fire pole gap when my kids and I stepped in and carried him straight to his dad. My kids were so upset, they set into the dad like the playground SWAT team; I didn't have to say a word.

Always wear helmets means for biking and some sports, not for jungle gyms. But you can't just stick a helmet on your kid and think he will survive every situation. School jungle gyms are made for school-age children.

About fifteen children a year are killed on playgrounds, and about ten of those accidents occur on home playgrounds. Don't let your children wear hoods, scarves, and clothes with drawstrings. Most of the children were strangled when their clothes got caught on some piece of equipment. The most deadly piece of equipment was the swing set.

How often have I heard parents say, "Just play on the swings. The monkey bars are too dangerous for you."

Falling eight feet from playground equipment onto dirt or insufficient padding is like smashing into a brick wall at thirty miles an hour. But more home-jungle-gym deaths come from swings.

School playgrounds have their share of injuries. When it comes to the 210,000 kids under fifteen who make it to the ER from play equipment, over half of the injuries happen at school. More than two-thirds were falls to the ground or onto other playground equipment. During school, 70 percent were falls to the ground, and 10 percent involved falls onto other equipment. Proper play surfaces are essential for both home and school playgrounds. Many parents don't want to pay for special play surfaces, saying they are for "sissies." This is absurd; do you really want a macho brain-damaged child?

If a school playground is well supervised, it is safer. About 40 percent of school playground injuries occurred when there was no teacher or assistant watching.

Reality Check

✓ Most jungle-gym deaths happen at home when parents aren't supervising the jungle gym properly.

Preventative Tips

No hoods, scarves, Popsicle sticks in the mouth, drawstring jackets, or drawstring clothes on the jungle gym. Most deaths occur from strangulation, and most happen on swings or slides when a scarf catches and the child is strangled. Supervision is the key.

Parental Worry: Is My Child Spoiled?

Keeping your children safe in this hostile world has come to mean the following:
- Creating a hedonistic games arcade at home
- Sheltering your children from all adversity
- Making sure that they are happy all the time
- Building up their confidence by telling them how fabulous they are
- Cushioning them from failure
- Watching them all the time (when they are past the toddler years)

How can anyone believe that this will prepare them for the outside world?

We are so afraid of the hostile world that we fortify the walls of our "castle" home and live "happily ever after" for a time. Then it all falls apart for our children as they go out into the wide world.

Kids feel entitled to live forever at "Disneyhome" and often aren't able to do anything else. (The real Disneyland has more challenges than many children's wired, person-free world in which the school challenges are sorted out by Mom and Dad.) They feel entitled to a cushioned life, can't cope with adversity, and freeze in new situations.

Keeping your children "safe" to this degree makes them unable to cope. This leads to depression and escapism. The parent's job is to prepare the child to cope in the world, not to cushion, protect, and keep him or her happy.

Failure is the step to knowledge and success. Babies fail all the time as they learn to walk and talk. As they get older, we take away the right to fail, expecting As all the time. This is a mistake.

Do not protect your children from, nor help out with, the following:

- Anxiety (unless it's chronic)
- Defeat in a game
- Bad grades
- Exam anxiety
- Personality conflicts with friends or teachers
- Boredom
- Bad luck (don't buy them a toy if they don't win the prize)
- Constructive criticism from teachers (and yourself)
- Responsibility for cleaning their rooms
- Homework: organizing, doing, and remembering
- Low-level conflicts (i.e., learning to get along with
  a variety of children)

I know it is hard to look at these "negative" things as good, but they are brilliant motivators. At first it will be hard for you to back off and allow your children to experience pain. A superficially happy kid is so much easier to live with, but a child who can cope, be motivated, and be innovative will be happier in the long run. That child will be easier to live with than one who behaves like a spoiled, demanding toddler who cries, "I want that" or "Give me that" or who ends up cheating on homework, or, eventually, medicating himself with alcohol and drugs to numb his exposure to the world and remain in a false state of happiness. Help your children to learn how to triumph over these difficulties with calm, constructive analysis. Ask them how they could avoid the problem the next time. They must be self-motivating (with a few reminders). But you could try role playing to help them learn to calm down and teach self-talk so they can reason themselves out of a problem or a conflict.

But don't stop them from experiencing negative feelings. Just help them navigate through them with "How can you make it better next time?" "What did you learn?" or "You might want to plan to do your homework earlier."

It takes children seventeen to fifty times to learn something new. This is going to be a long and painful-to-watch process, but it's the only way that you won't end up with twenty-five-year-old kid who lives at home and plays video games all day because he has not learned to persevere, be resilient, or even do his own laundry.

How the Perfect Child Becomes the Perfect Monster

Use this cautionary tale of a high school girl. If I saved the story's message until the high school section of the book, it will be too late to learn the lessons.

She looked like a movie starlet made up for her close-up when she walked into Starbucks with her mother at 7:00 AM. My children and I were waiting at the front of the line for our order to be filled. The mother kept elbowing her teenage daughter, very agitated. Suddenly the girl shouted to the barista, "Make my double mocha-mint venti latte before theirs [i.e., us]. I am late for school."

I was shocked, my kids were shocked, and the barista looked horrified.

The next thing I knew, the mother tapped me on the shoulder. "This lovely, beautiful, elegant young lady [i.e., her daughter] is late for school, so we need to pay before you."

I said, "*No!* We are going to school, too, but my children got up early enough not to have to rush."

I was furious and stunned speechless. Unfortunately, I couldn't muster the words to put this woman in her place. Now, at least, I have this forum in which to lash back. I supposed the girl is doomed, anyway, so I should not harbor the fury I feel now whenever I see a Starbucks. It wasn't Starbucks's fault. In fact, the barista even came over and apologized for the two. She was equally shocked by their behavior.

That mother and daughter are examples of so much that is wrong in today's society. Here's my top-five list:

1. Sense of entitlement
2. No consideration for anyone but themselves

3. A child unable to do basic tasks without mommy (i.e., such as ordering on her own at Starbucks)
4. No personal responsibility
5. Consumption (the girl gets a Starbucks latte every day)

They felt a supremacy over everyone else. They had complete disregard for others. There was never a thought of skipping the latte because she was late for school. Four dollars every morning of every school day was considered money well spent. At 174 school days, that's nearly $700.

When that girl eventually goes to college, her mommy won't be there to order for her. Where will she get $700 for her lattes? The people she meets won't appreciate being stepped on. Her roommate will hate her because she is a spoiled princess with no social skills or social conscience.

College administrations are reeling from the influx of helpless, entitled teens.

That mom undoubtedly believed that she was making her daughter happy and doing the best for her. She felt her daughter deserved to be admired by all. And in the process, that mom created a helpless, incompetent, needy monster. Give your school-age kids a chance to practice independence, accountability, and responsibility.

Replace Reward with Recognition

Tell your children that they have done a good job or tried hard and leave it at that. Don't give rewards for daily life. Working for rewards is fine, but a reward is not appropriate for going to the grocery store, doing homework, or being quiet during a parent's phone call.

Let your kids learn that some chores are nonnegotiable. Help them learn to do activities for the pure enjoyment, not for constant rewards.

Boys Versus Girls, at All Ages

This book could have been called *The Trouble with Boys.* Even the sweetest little boy who succeeds in growing up into a nice young man—for which your odds are great—will still probably visit the hospital emergency room a couple of times a year.

Boys are about 75 percent more likely to get into every kind of trouble than girls are. What is going on with boys! Testosterone and upbringing.

Most of the trouble (i.e., injuries and fatalities) is their own fault. (Or maybe it's yours for not teaching them the rules and enforcing them early so that the rules become second nature by the kids' teen years, when you aren't there and their thinking brains are on vacation until their twenties.).

Little boys are nearly 75 percent, on the average, more likely than girls to drown, have sports injuries, get hit by a car, be killed in a fire, or get hit on their bike. Teenage boys are more likely to commit suicide, to get killed while driving a car, to try drugs, to know where to get a gun, to get killed by a gun, to be in a gang, and to get in physical fights. Boys aren't as likely as girls to buckle their seat belts. Boys get bitten by rattlesnakes on their faces and their hands because they will pick up the snake. These are largely preventable, with just a little education and by rejecting the "boys will be boys" attitude and "you are a man now" ethos.

If you have girls, you could almost stop worrying until the tween years, when it is eating disorders, psychological bullying, binge drinking, self-mutilation, failed suicide attempts, and the most lethal: riding without seat belts in a car packed with drunk teens. But these are not common threats, just the most likely problems. And remember, it is usually one "bad" girl getting into lots of trouble, not all girls doing one thing bad.

Older girls make more unsuccessful suicide attempts, but little girls are more likely to shout when they are drowning or get out of a burning building while boys hide. Girls try drugs less often but can get in more serious trouble for sexual experimentation. The chance of a girl under fifteen being shot is almost zero, regardless of her background or where she comes from.

As teenagers, girls are more likely to be victims of kidnapping by strangers and sexual abuse by known and stranger predators. Girls get bitten by rattlesnakes on their ankles. Boys take more low-level risks and are more likely to have broken bones.

I have said that little boys are more likely to drown or to die in a fire. However, the significant factor is usually poverty. The same is true for older boys. Boys who are from traumatized or grossly disadvantaged families are at far higher risk than boys from average middle-class, "happy" families. But also in the high-risk category are rich boys with more money and arrogance than sense.

The high-risk groups completely skew the safety statistics when we are looking at the majority of boys. So if you hear a statistic that a certain percentage of children are in danger, you need to know if there is a high-risk group that makes that danger almost completely irrelevant to you and your child.

Parental Worry: Amusement Parks

"I am scared to take my kids to the theme park. I am putting it off until they are much older. Pedophiles, dangerous rides. Lots of kids end up in the hospital or worse from theme parks, don't they?"

I have heard this a lot, and my reply always shocks: "Book the ambulance for the amusement park." I am exaggerating some. "Kids *are likely* to go to the hospital from a trip to the theme park, but it isn't because of ride accidents, it is dehydration." Yes, thirty-two-ounce free refillable caffeinated soft drinks served up in character cups are to blame, not faulty rides.

Parents take their underfed kids to theme parks and buy them a supersized Sponge Bob drink container and keep refilling it for free with caffeinated soda rather than water. The consequences are steep: the children become seriously dehydrated. Caffeine drinks dehydrate. Kids may vomit and even pass out. Serious dehydration can cause death or at least hospitalization. Exhaustion is high up the list of children's injuries. You don't want to spoil the vacation. Give your child food and water at frequent intervals. Theme parks are remarkably safe when you look at the millions who ride the rides multiple times day after day.

Theme parks are some of the safest adventure activities you could ever do. Only thirty-five serious injuries result from 1.8 billion theme-park rides each year.

Faulty riders usually cause the ride accidents. Most rides are safe, more so in an amusement park than at a rickety touring country fair, as long as parents follow the safety rules. Warnings are everywhere, but parents still let their kids hang their arms out of the car or stand up.

Just because your giant three-and-a-half-year-old can pass the height requirement of the average six-year-old does not mean that he or she should be allowed on the ride. I have often witnessed cases in which dads are so proud that their child is tall, and therefore more manlike than his peers, that they push their young children on these thrill rides for older children. A tall, young child can get scared and try to get out of the ride, whether or not he is riding alone or with a parent. A parent must be strong and not give in to their taller-than-average child, or even the tween wanting to ride a teen ride. The child doesn't have the learning or the reflexes yet to ride the ride safely. The ride that sends up the danger statistics is the local fair's bouncy castle. Kids bouncing around, especially different ages allowed in together, bump heads, and the head bumps end up being serious concussions. It is not worth it.

Parents also should look at the condition of the rides. Is there yellow tape around one of the cars, meaning that it is out of use? If a car is out of use, then the engine and the other parts of the ride are probably not well maintained. Avoid that ride.

Most ride deaths and injuries do not even happen to young children; they happen to drunk college-age kids who throw their arms in the air and stand up on a roller coaster.

Preventative Tips

Keep your kids hydrated and fed at amusement parks. Caffeinated drinks are not okay. Seek immediate help from the park's medical care if there are signs of dehydration. Go beyond strictly following the height requirements. An extremely tall child of a younger age should not be allowed on a ride for older children.

Parental Worry: Razor Blades in the Halloween Candy

The Denver police put out this warning every year at Halloween: "Check fruit and homemade treats for punctures or foreign bodies that may have been injected, such as pins, metal needles, or razor blades. Allow your child to eat such items only if from someone you know and trust. Most treat makers are well intentioned, but it's not worth the risk."

Would I contradict the police? Where do our fears come from?

In a 1970 case, family members sprinkled a five-year-old child's Halloween candy with heroin to hide the fact that he'd gotten into his uncle's drug stash.

In 1974, Ronald Clark O'Bryan of Deer Park, Texas, put

cyanide in some Halloween candy and killed his son, Timothy. O'Bryan did it to collect the insurance money on his dead son.

And those two cases started the urban myth that police forces, the media, and parents across the nation live by today.

"But there must be more!" you might insist. No, there aren't. That's it for death by Halloween candy. Number of deaths from strangers handing out lethal candy: none.

What about razors, needles, and rat poison? They sound scary, but none of these will kill you. They really don't. A razor blade might slice up your mouth and hurt a lot, but it won't kill you.

What about the millions of sick and injured children from Halloween candy? Here are the findings:

James Joseph Smith of Minneapolis did put needles into Snickers bars and hand them out. One child was pricked with a needle when he bit into a candy bar, but no child was seriously hurt. Furthermore, this was in the year 2000, long after the urban myth had already become commonly accepted as fact.

In 1964, Helen Pfeil of New York didn't think that older kids should trick-or-treat, so she gave them steel wool pads, dog biscuits, and poison ant pellets, but she warned the kids not to eat them. She was charged with child endangerment.

That's it for Halloween "candy man" strangers. Again, we must look to the home itself.

"Mom, Dad, look, there's a razor blade in my apple!" These cases, although they hit the media with hourly coverage for days, have proved to be the work of the children themselves. And others have imitated, with razor blades and pins and needles—

usually to scare a sibling, not for public consumption. Parents who want their fifteen minutes of fame have also been the hoaxers, presenting found objects to the candy man–hungry press.

Just think of the years of Halloweens that have been ruined by the worry that our children would swallow a razor blade.

Candy itself is actually the true Halloween bad guy.

Candy is not good for you. Eating a cookie jar's worth of sugar a week is causing obesity, diabetes, and heart conditions in children that used to be found only in unhealthy adults.

Here is a scary candy story that happened during Halloween week at Disney World. On a Disney bus that morning, a dad was looking at his son, who was tired from a trick-or-treat party. I heard the dad say to the mom, "Let's find the candy store first and load him up on candy, or we will never get through the day." I thought he was joking, but his wife produced the park map, and they located the candy store for their first stop. That night the family was going back to the Magic Kingdom for more trick-or-treating.

One year, I let my elder daughter eat all the candy she wanted. It wasn't very much. Nevertheless, she got a terrible stomach ache. She didn't eat any Halloween candy the next year.

Being paranoid, last year I took the advice of a health official and put the candy away for two days to let any possible H1N1 virus on it die. (Actually, this is a good idea.) I hid the candy in the garage and explained why to my kids, who were scared of H1N1 beyond reason, so they readily agreed. Two days later, they had forgotten all about the candy.

If you're desperate to stop your kids from eating so much candy, maybe you can use a perceived danger to scare your kids off candy. "Don't eat the candy; it might be poisoned." It sort of is, given that it's so bad for us.

Preventative Tips

On Halloween, make sure that your kids aren't wearing masks that obstruct their vision or long costumes that will make them trip. Set the candy aside for two days to kill any germs it carries. Better yet, trade all that candy for a toy or give the hard candy to soldiers going overseas to help soothe their parched throats in the desert.

Middle School

During the middle school years—the tween years—the injury and death rates increase. There comes a point when all children must make their own—we hope right—decisions. That point should have started in nursery school or kindergarten, when you weren't there. You should not wait until the tween years to teach common sense.

Parental Worry:
Is My Child Watching Too Much TV?

Have you ever taken a long-distance flight? Jet lag is real, and it is unpleasant. Your body's clock becomes confused, and you don't sleep properly. TV jet lag is making your child stupid.

That is right, TV can have a jet-lag effect. More than half of the children in the United States have TVs in their bedrooms. Watching TV late is bad enough, but many of these kids fall asleep with the TV on. The light of the TV screen "fools" the body's clock into thinking that it's daylight.

173

"But the TV puts them straight to sleep," you object. "They don't watch it for more than ten minutes, and then they are out cold."

Important sleep and dream cycles are interrupted or missed if a child falls asleep with the TV on. Children will not retain what they have learned if they do not experience all the sleep stages each night. Falling asleep with the TV on means no deep sleep, so what they learn in school is not processed into long-term memory. They will forget what they learned for the test and for life.

So don't allow TVs in your children's bedrooms! It's tough, but you can do it.

Annual Number of Deaths by Accident, Homicide, and Suicide: Ages Ten to Fourteen

Motor vehicle	703
Homicide, firearm	175
Suicide, suffocation	137
Drowning	114
Other land transport	66
Fire or burn	64
Suicide, firearm	62
Undetermined suffocation	58
Poisoning	40
Nonland transport	30

Aside from sleeping with the television on, there are other issues about TV watching to be concerned about. The best data indicate that children should spend no more than an hour on a school night staring at a screen, be it television, a computer, or an electronic game. More than that seems to be okay on the weekends without having a negative impact on grades.

Preventative Tips

No televisions in children's rooms! When they do watch TV, try to watch it with them. Keep in mind that the vivid scenes they see on TV are more memorable than real life, and their minds interpret these scenes as experiences. Reality does not move at the pace of TV and movies. Real life can seem boring compared to television and electronic games.

Parental Worry: Eating Disorders

What frightens girls more than cancer, nuclear war, or losing their parents? Thinking they are "fat." About 80 percent of ten-year-old girls are afraid of being fat, and 80 percent of ten- and eleven-year-old girls have dieted.

The number one wish of tween and teen girls is to lose weight. The majority really say they are more worried about being fat than about losing mom and dad. They aren't being smart, mature, or right about this, but it is their belief, inculcated in them by our weight-obsessed culture and mass media and reinforced by four out of five of their friends. It is like a crazy religion; they believe it with all their being and, in some cases, unto death.

You might think, "Not my daughter." "Not my third- or fourth-grade girl." But many girls are skipping lunch or leaving the table during dinner to weigh themselves. The problem starts earlier than the tween years. Children as young as three and four years old avoid fat children. Preschoolers describe fat silhouettes as stupid, dirty, lazy, sloppy, mean, and ugly. Where do they learn these stereotypes? Even at age nine, nearly 10 percent of girls have vomited to lose weight. The statistics only get worse for girls ten and older.

More than half of girls ages nine to fifteen try to lose weight by exercising; just under half try to lose weight by eating less; and one out of twenty has tried diet pills or laxatives.

Other countries have known starvation—in the past and now. In the famine in the Netherlands after World War II, the Red Cross rushed food to the people who were eating 1,200 calories a day. This number of calories is considered semistarvation, yet many young people in the United States today try to eat only 500–900 calories a day. Half of the mothers I know are starving themselves; is it any wonder that their daughters are getting the message at such a young age? The basic Jenny Craig diet is 1,200 calories a day. Semistarvation depresses your metabolic rate, slowing down weight loss.

We provide girls with completely unrealistic role models at a very early age. The Barbie doll is a classic example. If she were life-size, Barbie would be six feet tall, 101 pounds, have 39-19-33 measurements, and wear a size 4.

In the film *The Devil Wears Prada*, which had a rare female heroine for teenage girls, the advice given was that dress size 2 is the new 4, and 6 is the new 14. Sizes 11 to 14 are normal for a woman and teenage girls, but they are being told that they need to grow up to wear a size 2! There is even a size 0; what message does this send—that you shouldn't exist?

Most fashion models are 23 to 25 percent thinner than the normal healthy girl.

When I was in college, an amazing actor friend of mine in New York constantly yelled at me to stop dieting. He was a handsome six feet, five inches tall and skinny as a rail. He pulled out his photo spread for the *New York Times* Sunday magazine and handed it to me: six pages of him in wigs, posing as a woman, modeling women's fashions. *Many photographic fashion models are extremely thin men who are made up to pass as women.* There are no captions to let people know that the models are men. It is impossible for young women to be thin enough to suit some designers, and now young girls dream that impossible, distorted dream.

Teenage girls can never be as thin as boys or men are, and there is no good reason that they should want to be.

At one time in my life, I was exercising six hours a day and eating only 800 calories a day. A nutritionist told me to start eating at least 3,500 calories a day of low-fat and high-fiber foods. I tried, but I could not eat that much food. I lost fourteen pounds in two weeks, and I was bouncing off the walls with energy because I was eating healthy food and exercising. In our society today, I wouldn't tell anyone to eat that much; most people would probably eat burgers, fries, and chocolate. You can eat right and turn your body into a calorie-burning machine, and you will be a healthy weight for your body type. Starving isn't going to do it.

Parental Worry: Extreme Sports

Skateboarding is an evil plot generated by orthopedic doctors to generate business and destroy my child's well-being. Actually it isn't. Really.

The number of fatalities per year due to skateboarding is forty-two, and that includes adults. But only two of those occurred in a skate park; one fatality was an adult. Compare that with the number of children—three—who die each year from a head injury sustained while playing baseball. Baseball, as I mentioned earlier, is considered the most lethal popular sport by the CDC.

None of us wants to lose our children or see them in pain and injured through a sport they love, but when it comes to the dangers of skateboarding, there is reality and then there's the perception of reality. It's a big difference.

It's true: kids fall a lot while learning to skate, and most injuries happen within the first week. But like most sports or any other worthwhile activity, skateboarding builds critical self-esteem, brings happiness, and teaches social skills.

Skateboarding can also help kids learn to take risks wisely. You can do almost anything *if* you follow the safety precautions.

How do I personally feel about skateboarding? I was a Midwestern daughter who married a playwright and spent most of my years immersed in the theater world in London. While I was writing this book, I watched my five-year-old triplets and my eight-year-old daughter take their first skateboard lessons. I can assure you that I was as excited as they were. So when, the next morning, one of my sons asked for a board of his own, I didn't blink. They would learn the skill and the safety savvy.

We simply follow a few ironclad rules: Skate in the skate park, not on the street or anywhere around cars. Always wear basic protective gear. This includes a helmet, wrist guards, and elbow and knee pads. They're easily purchasable, a necessity, and worn by some of the skate world's most notorious rebels—including Tony Alva, who is still hitting the parks with audacity even though he's over fifty.

I don't know whether my son will still be skating then, but I do know how much he enjoys it now. And so do I.

Reality Check
✓ Skateboarding in the street, especially without wearing safety equipment, is dangerous.

Preventative Tips
Frequent a skate park. Helmets, wrist guards, elbow pads, and knee pads should all be worn. Skateboarding must be kept in the skate park and never done in the street. Parents can control the risks and teach their children how to control their own risks yet do really exciting things in life.

Parental Worry: Winter Sports

We often think of winter sports as being extreme. Skiing a mogul, snowboarding, or the viciousness of ice hockey suggests risk-taking at its most cutting edge. Granted, fewer people, proportionally, take part in these sports than in others. But safety equipment has come such a long way that if you're properly attired, some of these activities can be fun, lifetime sports. Others that seem less risky, however, can cause later-life health problems.

Extreme sports are actually not the scariest thing. It is the tween-teen mentality, not the sports themselves, that makes extreme sports more dangerous. Even toddlers with their blankies are often seen in a ski-lift line ready to ski down a mountain, and they often show more sense than the tweens and teens do. Little kids ski without poles so that their hands are free to hold their favorite stuffed animal. I pulled my then three-year-old daughter Abby out of ski school. She got so good that the teachers were putting her in with the older kids and taking her up the mountain. I tried to find statistics on ski-lift falls, but I couldn't (and still can't) so I pulled her out of ski school. Knowing that my three-year-old was on a ski lift with four jostling tween boys and a ski instructor would have had me worried all day. I was worried about the four boys, not the lift itself or the skiing.

Skiing is not the terror that many parents imagine. Out of more than 12 million skiers and snowboarders of all ages, skiing a total equivalent of fifty-seven skiing/boarding days a year, only about 40 people die each year.

Bicycle deaths occur in 1 of every 3 million bike rides; swimming deaths occur in 1.32 of every 1 million swims. Men and boys are more at high risk. About 32 people a year die in tornadoes. Annual injury figures for skiing vary widely: between 12,000 and 18,500 children ages five to fourteen are treated in emergency rooms, depending on the year.

Parents worry about the dangers of skiing, but they don't think twice about the dangers of sledding. In ski towns, the locals joke that the ambulance comes to the sled hill more than the ski hill, and the statistics bear that out: the annual injury figures for sledding are that 15,000 to 23,500 children ages five to fourteen are treated in emergency rooms, depending on the year. It's true that more kids are sledding than skiing, but this is a high number of injuries for what should be good and simple fun. Many more sledding accidents are treated by pediatricians or aren't reported.

Parents who sled holding kids on their laps should use the new inflatable sleds to prevent back injury. You are your child's shock absorber, and you are not as bouncy as you were as a kid. Many a parent ends up needing back surgery from a sledding trip.

Both kids and adults should wear helmets on the sled hill as well as on the ski hill. Drunk young people and adults crashing into sledders cause many accidents.

Snowboarding is more dangerous than skiing, because fewer participate and the number of injuries is higher. Annually,

22,700 to 24,700 children ages five to fourteen are treated for snowboard-related injuries.

In 22 percent of skiing and snowboarding accidents, the injured person loses consciousness or has a concussion.

About 1,900 children age fourteen and under are treated for injuries in snowmobile accidents each year. Most of these result from being towed or when a sled or a tube turns over, strikes a fixed object, or is hit by another vehicle. About six children a year are killed in snowmobile accidents; this number is on par with toy-related deaths. Toys are safer than you think, but snowmobiles must be used with care and safety.

Tying your child's sled to the back of your car and pulling your kids around the snowy neighborhood as fast as you can go is just stupid.

Reality Check

✓ The real danger is not on the big hill where people ski, but on the smaller, sledding hill.

Preventative Tips

When skiing, figure skating, playing ice hockey, snowboarding, sledding, always wear helmets and layered clothing. And just because it's winter doesn't mean you don't need sunscreen and sunglasses or goggles.

Chapter Ten

High School

The Most Dangerous Time

This is what I have been keeping from parents of young children. The teen years are the most dangerous period for your children, as you can see by comparing the statistics on the next page with those in the previous chapters. The accidental deaths multiply by ten.

Kids who drive and ride in cars are at the highest risk. No only is there a high death toll from driving, but also a huge injury rate. These, like almost all car accidents, are due to human error and are avoidable.

Again, most of the other dangers are also avoidable by using good sense. But now it has to be your child's good sense, not yours. Laying down the law to kids this age is a fruitless exercise and will only make things worse.

Teenagers are out in the world, unsupervised. You aren't always with your children at this age. They are finding out who they are, preparing to go out on their own in life. You are still

Annual Number of Deaths by Accident, Homicide, and Suicide: Ages Fifteen to Nineteen

Motor vehicle	5,522
Homicide, firearm	1,892
Suicide	1,513
Poisoning	486
Drowning	320
Firearm	107
Other land transport	100
Fire or burn	86
Fall	83

their biggest influence, but you can't be a police officer.

Don't make rules for older children if you won't be there to enforce them—a teen needs to know how to think when you aren't there.

We are really doing the nagging, "Don't do that" lecturing thing backward. Our conversations with our small children are laced with "Don't do that. Stop! No!" Sometimes we can go on for twenty full minutes, criticizing our accepting six-year-olds. I call it the "parent monologue." We drive them to tune us out with all our unnecessary lecturing. They are at little risk in those years, so our criticism and instruction (i.e., nagging) should be minimal. We think we are helping, saving, and teaching our children, but it goes on 24/7. The poor kids are a captive audience.

Our kids arrive at their teen years sick to death of our nagging and hell-bent on trying out their freedom. They will soon be leaving the nest, and they vitally need to try out their wings. But this can mean that they do really dumb things, dangerously dumb things.

Teens don't think straight; it is physiological. They lose the ability to read people's expressions and emotions the way an adult or even younger child does, and this can make boy-girl relationships a real roller coaster and their dealing with authorities (like you) distorted. Other areas of their brain are kicking into action, but areas of the brain that control relating to other human beings and making certain kinds of decisions switch to low priority.

This is actually the time we should shout, "No!" 100 times a day. This is when we should be lecturing them. Their behavior warrants it. But this is exactly the point at which we must let go.

You had better already have set up those behavior patterns by now; seat belts and common sense have to come naturally, or they won't come at all. This is not the time that your kids are apt to learn common sense. It is too late to teach your children how to cope with all the new responsibilities, which range from being able to drive a car, not drinking, to managing money. You have to start early so that the right responses will be second nature at this age.

Keep talking to your kids—not lecturing, but listening and talking. Parents often think that they are losing control of their teens, and they are. That is a fact of life. Instead of trying to control your children more, be there as they experience new freedom.

Relinquishing control of your "baby" is hard. If it is any

consolation, the majority of teens say that they value talking to their parents. But now it has to become a dialogue and not the parent monologue that you have been inflicting on them. They are no longer a captive audience.

Death Watch: Planned and Accidental

Car crashes are the leading cause of death among teens; they account for 36 percent of all teen deaths. In addition, approximately 400,000 teen car occupants a year are injured badly enough to be treated in hospital emergency rooms. That is seven injuries every second.

Of teens' fatal car accidents, about 38 percent involve speeding, and 24 percent involve drunk driving. One in ten teens admits to drinking and driving once a month. One-third of teens admit to riding in a car once a month with a driver who has been drinking.

What are teens doing wrong? Inexperience and the inability to assess danger have a lot to do with many teen driving accidents. The longer they drive, the better they get. Teens, especially boys, are less likely to buckle their seat belts and more likely to drive faster. Alcohol is involved in one in three crashes. Of teens' fatal accidents, about 38 percent involved speeding and 24 percent involved drunk driving.

Teens—boys more than girls—often feel invincible and think that they have the inalienable right to be cool, so they decide that they no longer need seat belts. It's a stupid way to rebel against

Mom and Dad. In 2005, 10 percent of high school students (12.5 percent of boys and 7.8 percent of girls) reported that they rarely or never wear seat belts when riding with someone else. One in three teens admits to riding with a drunk driver at least once a month.

Most states now have laws governing how many kids can ride in a car with a teen driver. The following statistics from the CDC give you an idea of how crucial it is to obey these laws:

- A sixteen-year-old driving with one teen in the car is 39 percent more likely to get killed than one who is driving alone.
- A sixteen-year-old driving with two teens in the car is 86 percent more likely to get killed than one who is driving alone.
- A sixteen-year-old who is driving with three or more teens in the car is 182 percent more likely to get killed than one who is driving alone.
- The risks go up for seventeen-year-olds: 48 percent with one teen passenger, 158 percent with two, and 182 percent with three or more teen passengers.
- Sixteen-year-olds are the party at fault in 70 percent of their driving accidents.
- This drops to 63 percent for seventeen-year-olds and 45 percent for adults twenty-one to fifty-nine years old.

Besides not wearing seat belts, riding with too many in a car, and riding with a drunk driver, another really stupid thing that teens do while driving is texting or talking on the phone. Of course, many adults (who should know better!) are guilty of this, too, and many states are now passing laws against it.

Finally, when teens are in a car accident, they are extremely likely to totally wreck the car.

Shootings are the second leading cause of death among teens. About 135,000 guns are brought to school a day. Boys know where to find guns whether at home or at Uncle Bob's.

Suicide is the third-leading cause of death among teens—that is, teenage boys. Teenage girls attempt suicide but frequently fail. Teenage boys don't try as often, but they succeed more. Three girls out of every twenty will try. Few girls are serious; the attempt is usually more a cry for help than an actual desire to die. Girls are serious about self-mutilation and starvation dieting, but not so much with suicide.

Preventative Tips

Parents need to make smart behavior an automatic habit. Wearing seat belts starts from birth. It is not negotiable. Other things to teach your kids: Don't get into a car filled with kids. Don't get in a car with a drunk driver. Don't drink and drive.

Parental Worry: Should I Spy on My Teenager?

You want to catch your teenager lying, so you sneak a GPS tracker in the car. What are you trying to prove? That you have created a liar? What a bad parent you have been?

Teens are not home about 98 percent of waking hours, so it is hard to communicate, even in the best parent-teen relationship. Some parents think that they are losing control of their child, so they suddenly get strict just when they should be encouraging more independence. Surveys show that parents are still the biggest influence for teens: kids still care most what their parents say and think.

It is hard to undo years of no family dinner times, of conversationless family trips in the car, of TVs in the kids' bedrooms, of a total absence of knowledge of your children's friends and their families.

Parents were continually coming into our store wanting surveillance equipment and GPS trackers to spy on their kids. The only thing we sold from a "spy store" distributor was pepper spray in the shape of a lipstick or a pen for kids going away to college—the perfect gift? Instead of selling the parents GPS trackers, we gave them brochures and website information about family adventure weekends and vacations. That will do far more good than spying. So GPS trackers, no. Family bungy-jumping trips, yes.

Preventative Tips

Teens still need family dinners and family bonding trips. Try an adventure. Take the $250 down payment and the hundreds of dollars for minute-by-minute, real-time Internet GPS surveillance updates and spend it on some weekend bonding vacations.

Exception to the no-GPS surveillance rule: if you really can't stop worrying when your teens are out on their own but don't want to keep calling them to see if they have arrived somewhere safely, ask them if GPS or cell phone tracking is okay. You can have peace of mind and not need to keep calling them for reassurance, driving them crazy in the process.

College

Your "little baby" is going to college. You won't see a grown young woman or young man in your thoughts but that little kid there alone, going to class, falling asleep over his or her books in the student lounge or library, going to wild parties, throwing up in the toilet—arghhh!

Start preparing your child and yourself for college early—when he or she is a toddler. However, this does *not* mean over-programming! A friend of my daughter's, at age five, was doing Italian, French, Chinese, Chinese dance, figure skating, hip-hop, soccer, and Chinese cooking—plus a few more things I have forgotten. She also was required to write an essay perfectly each morning before she was given breakfast.

These parents were the greatest, hippest, most wonderful, and truly accomplished people, but they didn't see what they were doing to their child as a problem. The poor girl was nearly burned out at age seven. (Luckily, they adopted her sister and had to cut her schedule.) This is *not* the way to get your child ready for college.

The way to get your child ready for college is to practice independence.

Remember that your children have been on their own since the first day of kindergarten. You didn't go to kindergarten with them—at least, not most days. You had to teach independence yet be there all the time in case your kindergartner needed you. The same is true for your college kid.

Too many of today's children have never crossed a street on their own by the time they start driver's ed. You need to help them practice independence while you are still nearby to help out.

Annual Number of Deaths by Accident, Homicide, and Suicide: Ages Twenty to Twenty-Four	
Motor vehicle	5,712
Homicide, firearm	3,327
Suicide	2,497
Poisoning	1,193
Drowning	309
Fall	164
Other land transport	113
Fire or burn	110
Suffocation	87
Pedestrian	86

You won't let your children go to a concert in the next town in a car with a group of friends, but they will be leaving for college in a few months. Check out who is driving and let the kids go. You can monitor their progress for your state of mind through the trackers on their cell phones, if you absolutely must. But tell them that you are learning to let them go.

Don't forget to teach them some basic skills, such as doing laundry, cooking, paying for their own cell phones, and budgeting time as well as money.

Rising to attempt every challenge is more important than succeeding in a few areas. Keep in mind, when you are pressuring them to get straight As for college entrance: you don't want your child to "peak" in grade school, or even high school, or for that matter, college. You want them to have that drive to learn for life and "peak" when they are grown up.

If they do finish college, they might become a "twixter," a college graduate who, after graduating, lives at home or with a group of twixters, has no plans for a job, has no entrepreneurial intentions, has no plans to return to school for a master's degree, or maybe takes a job renting surfboards at a beach. That topic and age group are beyond the scope of this book.

Parental Worry: What Are the Odds That My Child Is a Porn Star?

Becoming a porn star is different from dropping out and sinking into a low-life existence. It often happens unwittingly to girls in college.

Talking to your know-it-all teen before she leaves for college can be tricky. The brilliant teen-advice author Karen Stabiner told me, "Be hip but direct on preparing your teen for college."

My survey of college graduates indicated the same. Colleges have great systems in place to help kids stay in college, such as driving services for underage drinkers and programs to help the partyers stop partying. Colleges do a great job offering advice to new students; they have great support systems and a protocol in place to genuinely help kids with their problems.

My college-graduate advisors came up with a list of must-knows for freshmen. Many students give in to flashing for a joke, and many teens have been exposed to "sexting." Teens should never flash or "sext."

Here's what you should tell your daughter. If you flash in public, you lose all rights to your image, and you can become the star of *College Girls Go Wild*, with no legal recourse. If you flash in private—well, there is really no such thing as "private," in this case, because everyone has a camera on his or her cell phone. You don't want an image like that to be the first thing that appears when prospective employers google you on the Internet. You can even lose your student grant for indecency "pranks."

Don't take anything seriously except your studying. Don't take roommate relationships, boyfriend-girlfriend relationships, popularity, and the party scene seriously.

Preventative Tips

Students sometimes do not take advantage of the help that colleges offer, or they need some extra advice. For example, although girls are coached to ask for a new drink when they have left theirs unattended, they do not always have the courage to do it.

Send your daughters off with what they need. Preparing them and being realistic does not mean approving of some behaviors. Date-rape-drug test kits and condoms are good things to give to girls. But don't give breathalyzers to boys. Boys use breathalyzers to see who can get drunkest fastest.

Parental Worry: The College Degree

How will your kids do? About 53 percent of kids who start college do not finish in four or even five years. Yes, I said over half won't finish college even in five years! So don't put all your retirement money into their college fund! The chances are fifty-fifty that they will spend the college fund money and have nothing to show for it at the end. It is easier to get a college loan than money for retirement.

Why are kids not finishing college? In some cases, the money runs out, and the student has to go back to work to save enough to finish college. Students on sports scholarship become injured, and they are out, usually by junior year.

There are other reasons for the failure to finish.

In London, a top private school had the best record of getting kids into Oxford and Cambridge Universities. Those kids spoke three languages, played on the winning field hockey team, played instruments in the orchestra, and had straight As in the advanced program. Every minute of every day had been scheduled, so they emerged from the private school as the most exceptional students in Britain.

The problem was that when they got to Oxford or Cambridge, they couldn't budget their time. They couldn't look after themselves. They could go wild with parties, however, and they had the money for drug experimentation. Young adults who have been overprogrammed as children don't have a clue how to organize their schedules, balancing studying time versus free time. It's a disaster.

Thus, this perfect private school that turned out perfect students had the highest first-year dropout rate from both Oxford and Cambridge. More than half of the students left.

Self-sufficient students with lesser accomplishments but who are organized fare much better.

College RAs, or resident student advisors, have told me that they observe consistent problems with entering freshmen. "It's always the rich kids who mess up," they say. College becomes two years of parties, until Mom and Dad cut off the funds for alcohol and recreational drugs and the school expels them for bad academics.

Another group that has problems are those who have had extreme discipline at home. Once they are on their own, they go wild. One young woman bought every drug she could find on the first day in the dorm; she overdosed by 4:00 PM, ended up in the hospital, and lost her student scholarship. Her parents had never allowed her to go to parties; she had had a 9:00 PM curfew on weekends, was never allowed to ride in cars with friends, and was always chaperoned when she went to the movies or on shopping trips. She had been completely cocooned out of fear for her safety, and it left her with no skills or self-control.

The final group that has problems at college are the helpless kids. Mom and Dad did everything for them, helped them with their homework, and fought their battles, so when they need to discuss their first paper for history 101 with the teacher, Mom flies out to help Junior talk about his paper. This is a new paranoid parent–generation problem that is proving to be a real difficulty for colleges. Some parents are even renting apartments in the college town so they can live there and be there for "their baby." And that is just what they have created: a baby.

It sounds as if I am blaming the parents, but the fact is that you need to do a lot more than just pay the tuition to get your child ready for college.

Preventative Tips

- One hundred thousand female college students report that they were too intoxicated to remember consenting to or resisting sexual intercourse.
- Remind your children, "You have wanted to be a grown-up since you were four, now here is your chance. Act like a grown-up!"

Chapter Twelve

The Recovering Worry Addict

How often have you heard someone say, "In my day, we didn't wear seat belts, we walked to school, and we played in the local creek." Ah, yes, the good old days! We ran free as children.

Twenty or thirty years ago, most of the media was local. But now, with many twenty-four-hour cable news networks and with Twitter, Facebook, and blogs, every local story becomes national news instantly.

In the good old days, we never heard about what happened to all the children in other cities or states. Problems existed, but we weren't aware of them. After all, we were just kids then, not paranoid parents with our ears to the ground.

Kids who rode in the front seat and went through the windshield in an accident remained a local story. We now have seat belts and car seats because kids actually did get hurt.

Kids getting concussions from falling off jungle gyms were not public knowledge at first. But finally the stories were shared. That is why we have great safe playground surfaces: to stop concussions.

The safety improvements in the past twenty or thirty years have been amazing. People now don't remember the large number of children who once died from measles. Car seats, seat belts, helmets, and pool fencing have significantly saved children's lives. Food control, though underfunded (and food labeling that is often more confusing than helpful), has prevented many ills.

We all survived, but the media were so limited that we never heard about the kids who didn't make it. More kids did not survive in the good old days.

We moan, complain, and worry more now, but this is the best time in history to live. We have never lived this long or made this much money. Crime is down, not up; drugs are on the decrease; and food costs are down to 15 percent of our take-home pay. Even in this time of economic uncertainty, we are still better off than we have ever been.

In twenty years (from 1987 to 2007), the death rate from accidents went down 45 percent for the under-fifteen age group. Bike injuries went down 73 percent. Fire injuries went down 62 percent. Pedestrian injuries went down 62 percent—but that is because parents have become too scared to let their children walk to school.

Many Americans live in cities with a negative crime rate, by national standards. Yet even when we live in one of the top-200 safest places in this country, we act as if we were on the front line of crime, as if we were in one of the ten most dangerous places to live.

It's a Great Time to Be a Parent!

We are not at war on our own territory; we can cope, for the most part, with natural disasters. We cope well with emergencies. We don't have terrorism on the level of many, many countries, but we worry about it as if we were on the front line.

What we do have is a gun-control problem, compared to other Western nations. This is a man-made, man-solvable problem. Even without actual gun-control laws, locking up guns kept at home would dramatically reduce the number of gun-related death and injuries of children.

We can stop being lazy in so many areas of our lives. It is a contradiction: we can be consumed with worry but do dangerous things for convenience.

Fatalities and injuries in the United States are overwhelmingly caused by human error that can be remedied. If it is such a great time to be a parent, then why are you still worrying?

Breaking the Habit: A Worry Rehab Program

I have some genuinely bad news for you. Your fundamental survival mechanism has been damaged. This addiction is harder to cure than the difficult task of giving up a physical addiction. Through no fault of your own, you have messed up the wiring of your survival mechanism. Survival is the core of your being. It is fundamental to humans, and some of us turn on the survival mechanism too soon and too often.

From physiological and psychological points of view, you need to reprogram your brain so that your middle brain doesn't flip on at the slightest concern. You need to rid your system of high levels of serotonin and other chemicals, and you need to filter information through a new priority rubric.

It is going to be harder than giving up chocolate. Here's how we are going to go about it.

Paranoid parents need to fight worry like an addiction. While working on the addiction, we also need to work on our behavior within the family. Turn off the worried nagging, and you will find that your kids turn off some of their whining.

Follow these few simple practices and stop worrying:

• Follow the four-step worry rehab program below.
• Don't be stupid.
• Don't be lazy.
• Don't be swayed.

Step 1: Realize That Worry Won't Help You

Worrying does not solve anything. Worrying is lazy. An hour of worrying is a whole lot easier than an hour sitting on the floor playing blocks with your child. Worrying is intellectually satisfying but totally passive. Nothing gets done. Worrying very loudly does not appease the god of dangers. Staying awake all night worrying only means that you will be tired and cranky the next day. Worrying feels like love, but it is self-indulgent.

Hovering anxiously does not create an invisible force field of safety around your child. What good do the following actually do?

- "I was awake all night worrying about the fourth-grade science camp three-day overnight."
- "I was awake all night worrying about the bully in my boy's class."
- "I was awake all night worrying about the plastic toys my kids chew on—is it the right kind of plastic?"
- "I was awake all night because the children are staying with their grandparents."
- "I was awake all night thinking about crazy Louise driving my kids tomorrow."

Don't confuse staying awake all night and worrying with love or with solving the problem. Worrying to this degree feels like love, but it is only wearing you down. If you think that this degree of worrying will get you to make some phone calls in the morning or fix the problem, then you are deluding yourself.

Figure out how to best solve the danger, write it down on a bedside notepad to do in the morning, and go to sleep. If the problem is unsolvable and is genuinely dangerous, then don't expose your kids to it. But don't agonize and lose sleep over it.

It is okay to call the babysitter if you forgot something vital to tell her. It is not okay to worry minute by minute during a dinner out with other adults. Worrying wrecks your dinner, convinces you that you love your child more than yourself, appeases your guilt, and feels like paying penance to God as a way of assuring divine protection of your child. But it doesn't actually help your child. This might sound obvious, but we do it anyway.

Your first step in calming down is to just say no to worries. Don't let yourself worry. At prenatal classes, many of us were taught to shout "No" when our thoughts were flooded with worries we could do nothing about. When you start to think about your worries, switch your mind to thinking about cruising up the Amazon; there is no evidence that piranhas have ever eaten a human. Piranhas and paranoia incite fear, but they are just little fish to be thrown back into the water. They are not worth the bother.

Broken bones will happen, children will get the flu, there will be scraped knees, children will be hurt by their friends and have to learn what a real friend does. You can be there to comfort and teach, but cushioning kids from learning about life and people will not help them.

Reality Check

✓ Percentages and frequency can sound high, but because the United States is so huge, the chance of most dangers happening to your child is small. Think of it in terms of money: if you have $74 million and lose $6, you wouldn't really care. Six children dying in 74 million and we go into panic mode.

✓ We don't generally use the rational part of the brains with our children. Each child is more valuable than one dollar. Losing one child is the biggest tragedy in the world, worse than losing a whole $74 million. But we have to learn some rationality so we don't cocoon our children in paranoia, wrap them in bubble wrap, or pack them in Styrofoam popcorn and lock them in their rooms until they are twenty. Do not call out the marines for a one-in-a-million danger.

Worry should not become an end in itself. You can solve the problem, or you can't.

You should not send your child into a situation that you think is dangerous and then go for coffee and commiserate with all the other parents who are sick with worry. Nor should you moan and cry to your spouse until your child gets home. If a situation is truly dangerous, your child should not be there.

> **WORRY LESS TIP:**
> Worry makes your life miserable enough, without worrying about the wrong things. Worrying about the wrong things leaves your child unprotected. Learn the right things to worry about, and reduce those risks.

Think *No, I will not yell "No!"* ten times before you say "No, stop that!" to your child—unless the child is going to die, hurt someone else, or suffer severe brain damage. (Helmets and seat belts are absolutely nonnegotiable.)

Preventative Tips

Broken bones will happen. Skinned knees and elbows are okay. Trips to the emergency room will happen. Your children missing you is okay. They will learn that you always come back. Your children will often behave better and follow rules better in a school group than with you. If your children refuse to wear hats and gloves on a cold day, they will learn very quickly to wear them. If your children forget their homework or their gym equipment, don't take it to them. Seat belts and helmets must always be worn. Activities that can cause death and concussions are not okay. Never worry alone, and never worry in a group—just as an alcoholic should never drink alone or in a group. Just say no to the next worry. Constantly saying no to your child will make him or her deaf to the word.

Step 2: Prioritize Your Fears

We want to fix everything, so it is a hard concept to accept that trying to fix every contingency can be a waste of time. The odds of some dangers are 1 in 10 million; other dangers are more frequent. That is easy to see in certain aspects of your world, but it's very hard for some parents to accept.

A woman we know didn't take a vacation for forty years because she thought something would happen to her house if she were away overnight. We would say that she is crazy or that she should work on her phobia, but for her, leaving home for a vacation was not an acceptable risk.

In the areas of home, work, and even relationships, we have perspective, but for some reason we just can't seem to have that kind of perspective about our children. It is so hard for parents not to be afraid that the one child who is going to get hurt will be their child.

You say, "If it happens to even one child, that is one child too many—and it could be my child." Any child injured is indeed a tragedy. One child dying is not trivial, but, as a risk, it is small.

Some parents speak of wanting to wrap their children in cotton balls and bubble wrap or never letting them leave their rooms from birth until they are eighteen. Newlyweds have come to me for advice, asking, "How can we possibly have children? The world is so dangerous now."

But if you spend two weeks in Las Vegas in July, is it really necessary to pack a snow shovel just in case there is a blizzard? Would you buy hurricane insurance if you lived in Denver? Can we get 1 in 74 million into perspective?

Step 3: Stop Nagging and Spending to Fix Dangers

Trying to fix everything seems completely justified, even if it means you are a neurotic wreck and not a happy parent.

Our mistake is that we see a problem or a danger, and we think, *Do something. Do anything. Just fix the problem! And fix it fast.* Then we feel a great relief that we have solved the problem or fixed the danger. Sometimes doing nothing can be better than rushing to a quick fix.

Baby helmets for walking can be more dangerous than letting the child learn to walk by falling. Many safety devices are more dangerous than the danger they are meant to fix. Any wooden toy is not better than all plastic toys. Substituting tiny cute little toys for Easter or Halloween candy can be dangerous; for instance, some kids assume that tiny erasers are candy and eat them.

On a national scale, this wariness causes millions of dollars in rush spending, without parents prioritizing or thinking of the best solution. Donations go not to the most needy causes but to the most vocal.

At home, we often speak before we think when we see a little danger, and we lecture our children, "Don't go there! Stop doing that! Slow down!"

Listen to yourself talking to your children. Catch yourself with every warning. So many parents can't hold off for twenty minutes without saying anything to their children that isn't a warning, a safety instruction, or advice. We nag, terrify, and bore our children. Preparing is good, but translating the fear into daily life is not. We nag our kids about every crack in the sidewalk.

This nagging translates into big bucks. We will spend money if that is what it takes, no matter what the odds, to stop one injury.

Look at your high-risk list. I am not saying that you should not protect your children from trivial and low-risk dangers, nor am I saying not to protect them from fantastically rare dangers. Just try to get your common sense working properly. Don't take down the potentially toxic plastic shower curtain if it means that water will get all over the bathroom floor and your child will slip on the tile and get a concussion.

Not every house needs a "safe room."

My research has taught me when to delete a "worry song" on my mental iPod, skip to the next track, or turn off "Worries FM."

Step 4: Learn to Cope with Random Accidents

Being afraid that an accident will happen will not stop an

accident from happening, nor will it make you better able to cope if one does happen. Our inability to cope with the thought of accidents and random acts is one of our major challenges as human beings. How do you learn to cope with the unknown?

Lesson 1: *Accidents happen. Your cool, rational frame of mind will get you on the lifeboat.*

My kids love *Titanic*: The Artifact Exhibition, which traveled around the country to nature and science museums and is now a fifteen-year exhibit at the Luxor Hotel in Las Vegas. You enter the *Titanic*, which is complete with the grand staircase (where Kate Winslet saw Leonardo DiCaprio in his tux), the state-rooms, and the promenade deck. There is even a warehouse-size part of the real *Titanic* and the pièce de résistance, an iceberg.

You and your children are each given the ticket of one of the real passengers, with his or her life story, and you go through the exhibit as that person. One of my children was given Miss Marjorie Charlotte Collyer, age eight, known as Lottie, a second-class passenger. Another got six-year-old Master Robert Spedden, a first-class passenger.

At the end of the exhibit, you find out whether "you" survived. Lottie's dad went down with the *Titanic*, but she and her mother made it to lifeboat fourteen. When Lottie grew up, she got married and had children. Robert too survived the *Titanic*, carried half-asleep to lifeboat three by his nanny, Muddie Boons, only to be struck by a car when he was nine, in one of Maine's first recorded car accidents.

You realize "firsthand" that nothing you, as a passenger, did would have stopped the tragedy. Anything you did would be as effective "as changing deck chairs on the *Titanic*," as the saying goes—whatever deck chair you had, you couldn't escape the iceberg. The *Titanic* passengers actually thought that they had selected the safest mode of transportation in the entire world.

Accidents happen, and we can't always prevent them. Wild worry and panic won't save you. You want to control all possible dangers to your child, but there is nothing you can do but wait until they happen.

You can't prevent a drunk driver from running into you. You can have everyone buckled properly, be driving defensively, and not be texting, talking on the phone, or even mediating a backseat fight. But sometimes accidents happen anyway.

Accidents aren't what you were prepared for. You can't *be* prepared for an accident, by definition. You wish you could be prepared for everything, but you can't anticipate the unexpected.

You see a monster semitruck bearing down on you in the rearview mirror. Its driver decides to pass you at ninety miles an hour on a slippery mountain road at a "no passing allowed" curve in the road. Panicking increases your chance of an accident more than keeping calm and coping with the danger. This happens to me a lot in Colorado. I used to get scared. Fear and worry have no place in coping with danger.

But you *can* be in the right frame of mind to cope with an accident.

Lesson 2: *Bad things happen. The more practice, the fewer accidents.* We want to protect our children. We want to shield them from bad things. But they need to know that bad things do happen, and they need to learn how to react in a real emergency.

When my kids watched the movie *Titanic*, they were scared. People die, kids die, cute Leonardo DiCaprio dies (that is, his character does). However, I had decided that the *Titanic*—my "edited," child-appropriate version of the movie—was a sterilized disaster that my kids needed to know about.

It is not appropriate to expose children to real death and dying without some coaching; otherwise, they can be traumatized for their entire childhoods. Americans were actually never shown the entire footage of the destruction of the Twin Towers on 9/11 (complete with crashing bodies, for example). French television showed it.

Kids do need to know about real dangers; and they can learn how to control themselves. When you practice staying calm, you are role-modeling this behavior for them, so they learn to stay calm, too. Establish a code word for fire drills and emergencies. When your children hear or say this word, they will know that a real emergency is happening and to listen to and follow directions immediately. They have to be taught that there are very bad consequences for not doing so.

A child can't decide to defy Mom in a moment of real danger by sitting down and refusing to budge when Mom says to hurry. Having to repeat yourself ten times before your children listen happens at least once a day, if not all day, but it can't happen in the middle of an emergency. A child can't have a temper tantrum about combing her hair if it means that you will miss the lifeboat.

With my family's drills or in real minor emergencies, I get to practice my stay-calm-in–the-face-of-danger voice, and I expect my children to listen immediately, not argue, and follow directions. I just say our code word, "Titanic," and they know how to firmly proceed. They knew what to do when we got stuck in an elevator or when the kitchen caught fire, and they would know what to do even for just a badly skinned knee.

You need to be in control, and your children must see and participate in that control. Then life's scary experiences will be as manageable as they can be. Your wild fears won't become your child's wild fears, and your children will feel able to take control in an accident.

Calm decision is what you need when there is an accident, not dithering worry-driven hysteria. Control means not being continually in a ramped-up state of anxiety. Teaching your children control and coping is more far important (and much more possible) than protecting them from everything.

How Much Does a (Preventable) Accident Cost Us?

Worrying about every little thing and not enough about the big things has a price. When you look at the costs of your misguided worrying habit, maybe you will be shocked into cool, appropriate action—no more nagging, no more unnecessary spending or stress, just efficient action.

If you replace worry with efficient action, you can prevent many accidents. In actuality, millions of parents worrying about the wrong things is a national economic disaster. This is important to you and your family, but it is widespread. Talk about trillion-dollar spending!

For children under fifteen, who are supposedly under their parents' control, there are 14 million who are injured badly enough to go to a doctor's office or an emergency room. Of these children, 92,000 become permanently disabled, and more than 5,500 die. These figures do not even include poisonings—only external injuries and deaths from those injuries.

The high number of accidents means that we are not paying attention to real dangers, even though we think that we worry all the time.

Did you ever ask yourself how much an accident costs? One broken arm or one concussion means real dollars spent and lost. Those costs add up and have multiple financial ramifications. And you won't believe the overall cost to you and all of us. Get out your calculators, please, students. Most people just present a health insurance card and hear no more about the cost. Some may pay a deductible of $60 for the doctor's office and $120 for the emergency room. For those without insurance, a broken arm or a dog bite has to be paid in full out of pocket: $300 here, $1,000 there.

But the medical bills we pay aren't the entire cost. When averaged out for all those 14 million hurt kids, the cost is $650 per child in direct medical costs. Figure in all the insurance company letters, the time off work, the time you spend on the phone when the billing is wrong, child care, the loss in quality of life for a while, and other quantifiable short-term losses. Before you know it, a few chipped teeth or a sprained ankle could total $11,650 for short-term losses as calculated by SafeKids, a nonprofit coalition of health and safety experts, educators, corporations, foundations, and governments formed to educate parents on preventing injuries to children,

We are so happy that our child survived a broken wrist on the trampoline that we never add up the cost of missed soccer, or extra tutoring for missed schoolwork, physical therapy, time off work, and chronic residual problems later in life. Trampolines are really dangerous under all conditions.

Think about a fall on the ice rink because your daughter tried the double-toe loop at age seven instead of waiting until she turned ten and had the solidly developed ankles needed to make the big jumps. Perhaps there's not much fallout at the time, but when she's in her thirties, the damage from that "little" fall can turn into chronic back pain, endless treatments, medication, surgery, and a bad quality of life, just when she should be enjoying her young family. Instead her health is all downhill, with pain, increasing expense, and disability. The fall wasn't an accident—it was a result of not following the safety guidelines for the sport.

When you factor in chronic effects over a lifetime, with its family ramifications, you can be looking at a $1 million loss for each injury.

The Best Get-Rich Quick Scheme There Is

The worst thing is that 90 percent of all of these deaths and injuries of children under age fifteen are preventable.

If we were to get serious about the few big preventative measures—seat belts, helmets, appropriate supervision, smoke detectors, and sports-safety rules—we and our country would be billions of dollars richer.

Let's look at school injuries. About 2.2 million kids under fifteen get hurt at school each year, and the average cost of medical treatment per case is $1,000. That is $2 billion just in medical bills. When you factor in lost quality of life and future earnings, the bill could come to as much as $70 billion. Probably $60 billion of that would be preventable with safety measures that we are too lazy to follow. Are you willing to pay for change?

According to SafeKids, for every one dollar spent on a bike helmet, thirty dollars are saved in direct medical costs. So pay the thirty-five dollars for a good helmet, or donate one to a kid who can't afford it. For every one dollar spent on car seats, thirty-two dollars are saved in immediate medical costs. For every one dollar spent on smoke detectors, sixty-nine dollars are saved in medical costs.

For spending a little, we end up with safe, unhurt kids and save a lot of money in the process. Talk about getting bang for your buck. Stop spending a fortune on toddler-walking helmets and GPS systems for babies and buy and use the things that really stop the majority of accidents. Concentrate on a few safety fixes—using simple safety devices like helmets and seat belts, watching your kids, following sports safety rules—and stop worrying about all the improbabilities. Think of what all the money we save could do for healthcare reform in this country.

Enforcing Your Safety Rules

There are two sources of opposition you can expect when you try to enforce your safety rules: your kids and other parents.

"Bullied" Parent 1: Kids

"Mom, you're ruining my life. You never let me have fun. All the other kids get to [fill in the blank]."

Be prepared to hear this complaint from your children about many different things. The fixes are few, but you must enforce certain expectations. You can't rely on your spouse, your parents, or your children's teachers to get tough with your children. It's up to you.

Your kids will not just "grow out of" doing dangerous things when they are old enough to understand—they won't understand until they have kids of their own. There are not a lot of rules, but you have to stick to them.

I know that my son shouldn't Rollerblade down the block. I know what is best for my kids. But sometimes I don't enforce my rules. What goes wrong? As parents, we often sell out our standards under the least pressure. Humans try to find the easiest way to do things. So if children whine or throw a fit, parents naturally look for the quickest solution, which can mean giving in.

I am a "bullied" parent. I am "bullied" by my kids. The parents of my generation are worriers, fanatically obsessed with our children, but after a few whines, we crumble, just to make life easier for fifteen minutes. Have you ever heard yourself say any of the following?

"All right, just skip the helmet."

"Oh, stop whining. I know the seat belt is twisted.
   Just skip it."

 "Here, eat the whole chocolate bar."

"Go ahead, jump in the shopping cart."

"Okay, I know you are hungry—Happy Meals for dinner."

We buy a moment's peace at a high price. We might give the danger of doing it a passing thought, but we think we can beat the odds.

Soda for breakfast; no seat belt during the ride to school; I forgot the life jacket, so we'll borrow some floaties. We think we can cheat death—our kid's death. We think we can get away with it just this time. But "just this time" happens a dozen times a day. Parents, we need to grow up! There are real consequences for not doing so. There are just some things that we have to make our kids do, but we often don't have the courage to stand up to our kids. We may nag them nonstop, but we don't enforce what really counts. Stopping the danger means enforcing a very few safety rules—no cheating.

You may nag all the time, but actually, many parents only make their kids do homework. (If only my children were as in awe of their teachers as I am.) Only one in ten parents has the strength to actually stand by the helmet rule.

There are three versions of "Mom, you're ruining my life": the six-year-old's version, the ten-year-old's version, and the sixteen-year-old's version.

The six-year-old's rationales are the following:

1. Older siblings get to do it.

2. Someone has done it on TV—as a stunt.

3. The slacker mom next door lets *her* kid do it.

At this age, the dangers are still physical. You are still trying to save your children's lives because they don't have the judgment yet. It is not time to let go of the reins entirely and let them start exploring the wide world.

The ten-year-old's rationales are the following:

1. Double digits in years give children the illusion that they are teens.

2. Everyone on TV does it.

3. "My friends won't speak to me if I don't do it."

4. It's cool.

At this age, the dangers have just shifted to social and emotional. Parents will have a harder time defending their positions, but even more strength is necessary now. Those are not valid reasons. Freedoms can be earned with demonstrations of good judgment.

The sixteen-year-old's rationales are the following:

1. Everyone else is doing it.

2. "I have my license, so I can go where I want."

3. "I pay my own cell phone bill."

Sorry, parents, it's too late for discipline now. Kids of this age will be demonstrating their independence, and they *need to*. The first time they drive alone shouldn't be at college.

Do not nag. Be clear about expectations that are nonnegotiable. Self-talk—that is, tell yourself, *I am the boss. I am the boss.*

"Bullied" Parent 2: Other Parents

Then there are the attitudes of other parents. Do you stand up for what you believe in when parents look at you as if you are a paranoid nut case?

I absolutely hate this expression, but being the worried parent means you are the "poop in the punch". Be prepared to be treated like a party pooper or a know-it-all for the next eighteen years. Although you may see yourself as the brave one who speaks up on behalf of many parents, you will be viewed by some parents as killing everyone else's fun when you say things like the following:

"Do you have booster seats?"

"Do you own guns?"

"One chaperone isn't enough for twenty-five children."

"There's lightning outside."

"Curfew at ten."

"Did you check the coach's references?"

"No candy. No soda."

"No PG-13 movies!"

"Sorry, they can't go on the trampoline."

"Will there be boys there?"

You are the whistle blower. You're the "snitch" who becomes more hated for reporting the bully than the bully you turned in. How dare you suggest that a bouncy castle should be chaperoned and not a free-for-all. Other kids hate you, the parents and authorities at fault hate you, and your family hates you. You dared to speak up.

You are just trying to keep everyone safe.

Sixty Cub Scouts and their families are at a rally. Eleven little boys have piled onto a toy wagon, and big boys are launching them down a steep hill on a concrete path. Do I go up and humiliate my boys in front of every boy in school, or do I let them get hurt?

On the second launch, the boys crashed in a pile, with my son Zach on the bottom. He had badly scraped knees, but no concussion. Twenty boys surrounded my son. "He is brave. That is too dangerous!" they said. The boys took the wagon and put it away so that no one else would get hurt. They knew that it was dangerous, and they had been looking for a parent to put it away. But no parent was brave enough to "spoil the fun."

We all want to know what safety battles are worth fighting for. Armed with the facts, you will know what to stand up for, and maybe others will join you. Blame this book for your need to solve a problem.

A Brownie mom once used one seat belt to buckle four kids in the back of her car for a 100-mile trip on icy roads in a blizzard to Scout camp. She stuck her six-year-old in the front seat with the broken seatbelt. I saw four other mothers look terrified, but they said absolutely nothing. They didn't want to look not "cool." They met at Starbucks and worried there about the three-hour drive. I drove my own daughter to the camp. But I wasn't brave, standing up to the mother. I got lucky, having an excuse that we had to go see my kids' grandmother on the way so I would drive my daughter. Faced with the decision on the spot, I would have probably given in like the other moms did. But I did report her later and she was put on the "not approved to drive" list for the next trip.

I adored camp as a kid, but I hate it for my children. I realize that I sound pretty paranoid here. Camps do not have to report statistics, as they protect the confidentiality of "injured children" by not revealing their names—that's convenient for them. I let my daughter go, but I also went as a chaperone. I knew that a bear would walk through camp at 2:00 AM every night—a *real* bear, five feet away from twenty little girls. I don't sound so paranoid now, do I? What sense did it make to let her go just because I was going to be there? Did I really think I could wrestle the bear?

The bear did indeed come and "hang out" by the tents for half an hour. All it would have taken was one capless tube of toothpaste to attract the bear and we would have been the bear's 2:00 AM snack. What was I thinking? Then I found out that the organizers lied on the safety report to the Girl Scout Council. Did I turn them in? No. The girls also went on night hikes—six-year-olds chaperoned by thirteen-year-olds. The kids survived the midnight hikes because the paranoid moms (me included) chaperoned and located the four lost girls in minutes. But we just got lucky against the bear.

This is life, real life. There are no do-overs.

When a mother told me, "There are six kids coming, and we have a trampoline. It'll keep them busy for hours," I didn't say anything. I didn't want to look not cool and not hip.

When we don't speak up, we beat ourselves up, worrying aloud for hours and driving our friends and our spouses crazy from having to listen to our worry and remorse. This is while it is still going on, while we could still stop it.

Being a parent is not a popularity contest that you try to win with your kids and with other parents. Commit to fixing the dangers and stick to that without swerving. Be the parent.

Warning: Your popularity makes you give in instead of standing up to keep your child safe. Grow up and be a parent.

If something is dangerous, don't let your children do it. There are other Scout trips. There will be other sleepovers. ATVs are not essential. A parent needs to chaperone. Giving in to the pressure of "hip" parents when you know that you are letting your kid do something really dangerous is unforgivable. Stick by your standards. It will pay off in the long run.

What Are Those Parents Thinking?

Don't strive to be an average parent. Average parents do the following:

- Don't know how to buckle their child in a car seat properly (72 percent)

- Give their kids two or three sodas a day (72 percent)
- Don't make their kids wear helmets (80 percent)
- Don't feed their kids healthy food (98 percent)
- Eat more than half their meals out, usually at fast food places (more than 50 percent)
- Have guns at home that they leave unlocked and loaded (more than 50 percent)

Maybe you do have cause to be fearful—if so, it's not paranoia. Average parents who do these stupid things carpool with you, are Scout leaders, can be the parents of your kids' friends, and can be responsible for your kids at an adventure park or a poolside birthday party.

Don't look to the "herd" when you're making safety decisions about your child. "If seventy other parents are letting their kids skate without helmets, it must be okay." No, it sometimes is not okay!

Reality Check

✓ More adults than kids go to the emergency room for eating dirt; in other words, there are some very stupid parents out there. Most of us fall into the "average" category in too many areas.

Preventative Tip

Don't leave your children under the care of average parents. Take this book with you to morning coffee and show the other parents how shocked you are at reading this. You can blame me, but give them a reality check.

The Parent Cop

"Lady, that will be a $100 fine" or "Your court appearance date will be June 4. Floaties are illegal in this state." It sounds like a cop, but this is the way I would like to speak to some parents.

I went from being a paranoid mom to being a vigilante mom when I learned all the right things to worry about and saw other parents letting their kids do something dangerous. I see so many really smart parents doing so many really stupid things. I just wish I could issue a kid-safety violation ticket when I see such outlandish incidents of total endangerment.

Usually the parent offenses come from sheer laziness. The offenders are not necessarily slacker parents, "bullied" parents, or free-range parents. They are all of us on a bad day. The offenders are the Brownie troop leader, your neighbor, and your child's best friend's parent. I don't want to have to lecture my best friend not to drink at a kid's birthday party because she is going to be driving my child home. So it's easy to just turn a blind eye when we see kids in a dangerous situation.

What do you do when you see other parents—strangers or friends—doing something totally insane that puts their children in real danger or who behave in a criminal fashion or let their children behave frighteningly? I once watched a stranger smack her child in the grocery cart fifteen times during checkout. I stood open-mouthed in total disbelief and did nothing.

A new mom had her newborn in the sun for an hour with no hat. Showing off her beautiful baby was more important than protecting her baby from the sun. The baby girl probably received a quarter of the most serious sun damage in her life in that hour. All the ruin was there for future skin cancer or other skin damage, but I sat there, appalled, with a friend who is a doctor as well as a mom, and we cursed ourselves for saying absolutely nothing.

Recently, in Colorado, a pregnant mom with her toddler in tow saw a little boy torturing a cat in a public park. She asked his mom if he could stop it because he was genuinely injuring the kitten. The mother of the violent child beat up the "interfering" pregnant mom and is in jail for first-degree assault. As parents, we can't police other parents. I say we need parent cops.

I wish that a parent cop could issue a citation or a ticket to offending parents. If there were parent cops, I wouldn't have to cringe in silence, leaving a child in real danger, nor would I have to confront the parent.

Not all violations are a matter of life and death, but they still deserve a $100 penalty. Think about it: stopping a sugar addiction would save the parent thousands of dollars in dental work, behavior therapy, and health problems. So a $100 fine would be getting off easy.

Britain is considered a "nanny state." If your child skips school one day, you can end up in jail. If you keep your child out of school for an extra day at the end spring break, you will be fined $150 and your child can be expelled. Britain's school funding is based on attendance, and the British firmly believe that children can't learn if they aren't in school.

Here are a few of my favorite proposed fines:

- $1,500 for giving a soft drink and a candy bar to a tired toddler at a school play when the rest of the audience is trying to hear their little, inaudible actors above the din of the sugar-loaded monster child. (This amount is half the cost of three root canals for children.)
- $30,000 for letting a five-year-old play for an hour on an escalator so the parent can get shopping done. (This amount is the cost of an amputation.)
- $200 annually for letting your kid skateboard during evening rush hour down the middle of a dark street, with or without his helmet. ER doctors call helmetless skateboarders and motorcyclists the walking dead.
- $10,000 for having a few drinks at a child's birthday party, then throwing half the kids at the party into the back seat of the car to rush them all home.
- $20,000 for going to the hot tub and forgetting that you are the designated watcher for a ten-minute shift for five toddlers in a pool.

Most of these fines are too low, because we are talking about real dangers with serious consequences. The parents who do these things aren't bad. Many are friends (or former friends) who told me their near-escape stories. We have all done stupid things.

Reality Check

✓ We usually just turn a blind eye when we see kids in a dangerous situation. Whether it is watching a new mom keep her newborn exposed to the sun for an hour or seeing a parent smack a kid in the grocery store, what can we do to help? (Hand them this book.)

Preventative Tips

If only there could be parent cops who would fine parents for violating basic safety rules. Call child services if you see a serious offense taking place. Child services gets five calls a minute, and one in five turns out to be serious. Err on the side of caution.

Restoring Your Common Sense

By practicing not overreacting, by reacting to the right worries, and by cutting down on quick jumps to fix dangers, you will slowly stop releasing all those nasty stress chemicals into your system. You can stop the ever-escalating worry cycle.

Life should not be like a war movie in which you expect every phone call or ring of the doorbell to be an announcement of death. You shouldn't feel fear and trepidation all the time you're with your children, nor should you feel fear and worry whenever they are away from you. Life can sometimes feel like that on a bad day, but you are doing it to yourself. Your child is not dodging guerrilla troops on the way home from the market with a tiny flask of fresh water. (There are children who are. Let's not forget them.)

When you feel worried, go for a walk with your kids or leave them with someone and go for a run on your own. While you walk or run, figure out what is or isn't the danger.

The Miracle Cure

For those of you still looking for a miracle cure to your worries, there actually is one. I have saved it until last, sort of.

For the umpteenth time, consider the seat belt and the helmet. I keep talking about this because 90 percent of children's deaths and 70 percent of their serious injuries would be prevented if parents simply buckled up their children, used the correct child seat, or made sure that their children wore helmets for the relevant sports.

Helmets and seat belts—THAT IS IT!—the solution to most of your worst fears. It's that simple! If you are doing helmets and seat belts right, then take a deep breath and relax just a little, please. (I know you probably won't.) Put down this book and grab skateboards and helmets and go have fun with your kids, or go play on the school playground. You can stop warning them that danger lurks around every corner. Let go of 90 percent of your anxiety right now and have a great, fun life with your family.

The Recovering Paranoid Parent

After years of researching my worrying and yours, has my journey had any impact on me, one of the most paranoid parents I know? What about risk-taking? What about enjoying my kids? Did reading the endless numbers and statistics bring my common sense back in line with reality, banishing my misguided perception of reality.

Let me tell you a story. My kids and I were taking a plane trip, returning from fall break in Orlando, Florida. Don't get me started on the times the airlines have put my kids and me in single seats spread throughout the airplane! All my kids were sobbing and scared of being separated from me and each other. I was desperate. So as I walked away from the check-in desk, I muttered, "Hmmm, I know you've done your best—thanks . . . Kids, I guess, guys, Mommy will have to put this into the book I am writing." As we stepped aboard the plane, the check-in girl ran up and handed me five new boarding passes with us all seated together in a block, three in front, two behind. I know that this was "cheating"—but oh, the things we do for our kids! (If an airline does seat your child away from you, next to a stranger who won't move, hand the stranger a throw-up bag and say, "Can you have this ready for him? He always gets air sick." Flight attendants say that this works every time.)

Anyway, the boys were in the row behind me. The woman next to them asked, "Are they twins?"

"Triplets, actually," I replied.

She then said, "My triplets are in the row behind me, but they are eleven. I think we live near each other. I am the treasurer of the Denver multiples group. Do you mean that you just had triplets?"

"Triplets plus one."

"Oh, my God, at Disney World! Who helped you?"

"I was on my own with them, but they know the rules, and most of our time was on the Disney Cruise."

"Oh, my God, you did that on your own, too?"

"Yes, we had a great time," I assured her. "We swam with dolphins. We snorkeled out to see Mickey underwater but only made it as far as Underwater Minnie. We did the water park. We had so much fun."

"But weren't you worried every second?"

I couldn't believe my reply. "I didn't worry at all."

The kids and I knew what was potentially risky and how to cope with those possible dangers. We did things that I thought were adequately safe. And we did encounter activities that in the old days would have driven me to a worried, nagging frenzy: swimming at a beach, snorkeling with kids and in shark infested waters, the possibility that the boat would sink or that the kids would fall overboard, the chance that they would get lost in the theme park crowd or that pedophile Mickey would approach my children, the possibility that we would get H1N1 or that the plane would crash . . .

Our tales of the vacation were not the negative stories we used to recount after holidays (e.g., we got bit by baby jellyfish and survived; the boys came home with strep; dozens of kids got lost on the beach day—not mine, and it was a chaotic but fun mess for lunch). Normally we would fixate on the bad things from the vacation or the bad things from the school day. But a calmer mom means positive kids who know how to take risks, who know that something could go wrong but who are in control of their lives and their moods.

"We had a blast."

I am no longer a paranoid parent.

When the phone rings, I still check it to see if it is about my kids, and it often *is* about my kids—but it is usually that they have forgotten a bit of homework or their gym shoes—which I now won't bring to them. But my stomach has stop doing flips when the phone rings.

Knowledge does help you to reduce your worries, put things in perspective, and fix the fixable so that parenting can be fun again. You are a recovering parent, you are seeking help, and you may still get nervous. Reading this book, you now are in control.

Reality Check

✓ Fixing dangers works, but accidents do still happen.

Preventative Tips

Breathe more easily. Stop yourself from nagging. Enjoy your kids.

Statistical Sources

A Note About Statisical Sources

This book pulls together the top research so the parent doesn't have to look up hundreds of reports, some of which are reliable and some of which are not.

Even though this book contains many statistics, your attitude toward statistics should include the highest level of suspicion. Be wary of statistics. One thing that will make you really smart in judging statistics is to know the difference between *relative* and *absolute* statistics. Always look for the absolute statistic.

For instance, you might read that the number of victims of something has "doubled"—that's the relative statistic. In absolute terms, however, this can mean an increase of 5 to 10, of 50 to 100, or of 5,000 to 10,000. Five more victims a year is a lot less to be concerned about than 5,000 more a year, yet the term *double* masks this difference.

People who want to puff up their findings will use relative statistics; advertising is rife with this practice. Have you ever heard the claim that decaffeinated coffee has *half* the caffeine of regular coffee? A 50 percent reduction in caffeine sounds like a lot, but that's the relative percentage. The absolute percentage is actually only 2 percent, because regular coffee contains 4 percent caffeine and decaffeinated coffee contains 2 percent caffeine. Yet the claim is not a lie; 2 percent is indeed half as much as 4 percent.

Statistics are summaries. There are two "kinds" of average. One is the "mean" when you divide the total number in half. But in gathering statistics, you may not have a well-shaped bell curve. Days of collected data could be 10, 10, 5, 13, 150, 8, etc., so the distribution is skewed by the 150, and the mean doesn't show the central tendancy. So the second kind of average is the "median," which will show the central tendancy. Summary numbers don't add up because of these methods so please refer to the documents quoted for the explanation of the margin of error in each study.

The newest statistics are not always the best. It takes a couple of years to gather all the information together from all the sources across the country to come up with the true figure. Running trend surveys, like youth drug-use surveys, take meticulous grouping, testing, and analysis to come up with results that are fairly accurate. Twenty years is the scientist's benchmark requirement for making sound pronouncements and predictions. For instance, many doctors will not yet make predictions about the fate of extremely obese children because that condition has not been around for twenty years.

Sometimes data just aren't available. You can't give certain foods or drugs to a test group of children or pregnant women to see the overall effect, because the intervention can adversely affect the health of the participants. You can't lock up a test group of kids in a room for twenty years to see how they do being bubble-wrapped in a sanititized environment away from the world.

A new twenty-year survey is about to begin, studying 100,000 pregnant women and their children. This will cost several billion dollars to get sound data, which we won't have for twenty years or more.

Thus, only the most stable statistics were selected for this book. Emergency room statistics tabulate with accuracy. Reliability in statistics on the cause of death is continually improving. The Centers for Disease Control (CDC) is the ultimate source for that data.

On the CDC website (National Center for Injury Prevention and Control, Office of Statistics and Programming), you can input your search criteria—for outcome (death or injury), cause (from dog bites to self-harm, over twenty categories), age, race, sex, and year—to get the accurate statistics for recent years. http://www.cdc.gov/injury/wisqars/index.html is the link. WISQARS means "Web-based Injury Statistics Query and Reporting System." For instance: insect bites and bee stings that made it to the emergency room, ages birth to four, Hispanic, and girls. Up comes the number 9,227 for the most recent year with complete data, which is 2008, out of 2,534,453 million Hispanic girls under age five. You can find out how risky the primary dangers are specifically for your child by inputing their sex, age, race, and even state if you use the mapping function.

Another data source is the National Electronic Injury Surveillance System (NEISS) All Injury Program, operated by the Consumer Product Safety Commission. There is also Safe Kids Worldwide, a global network of organizations whose mission is to prevent accidental childhood injury, which is a leading killer of children up to age fourteen. More than 450 coalitions in sixteen countries bring together health and safety experts, educators, corporations, foundations, governments, and volunteers to educate and protect families. Safe Kids Worldwide is a nonprofit organization with headquarters in Washington, D.C. (1301 Pennsylvania Avenue N.W., Suite 1000, Washington, D.C., 20004.) Safe Kids is a bit like Paranoid Parents, but without my lecturing and attitude. I have included the CDC's most recent data for all age groups for accidental deaths and accidental injuries. Accidents are our chief concern as parents, for these deaths and injuries are largely avoidable. The numbers may be rounded off and averaged in the text. The tables give you the precise numbers.

In the three years that this book was being researched, many agencies changed their method of reporting data. Databases are now searchable online instead of all studies being in a printed form. Thus, I have sometimes cited these databases and not specific printed studies. The searches are customized and individual, up-to-date, and accurate.

For data that is widely available on several sources, I have tried to provide the most easily accessible source. All Internet data was last accessed in May 2010.

Sources by Topic

Injuries and Fatalities
Centers for Disease Control, National Center for Injury Prevention and Control, Office of Statistics and Programming.

Web-based Injury Statistics Query and Reporting System (WISQARS™) is an interactive database system that provides customized reports of injury-related data.

Consumer Product Safety Commission, National Electronic Injury Surveillance System (NEISS) All Injury Program: http://webappa.cdc.gov/sasweb/ncipc/mortrate10_sy.html. Click on link for fatality and injury searches.

Homicide, Suicide, Maltreatment, and Abuse Statistics: Breakdown for Demographics and Trend Analysis
Snyder, Howard N., and Melissa Sickmund. *Juvenile Offenders and Victims: 2006 National Report*. Washington, DC: U.S. Department of Justice, Office of Justice Programs, Office of Juvenile Justice and Delinquency Prevention, 2006.

National Center for Juvenile Justice
3700 S. Water Street, Suite 200
Pittsburgh, PA 15203-2363
Suicide, injury, deaths, and rates per 100,000, all races, both sexes, ages 15–19. http://webappa.cdc.gov/cgi-bin/broker.exe.

Marketing and Research Firm Polls and Analysis of Family, Tween, Mother, and Generational Trends
Intelligence Group Reports: http://www.youthintelligence.com/.

The Mom Intelligence Survey, the Mom Intelligence Report, the Cassandra Report.

Accident Prevention for Children: Child Dangers Data, Explanation of Trends, and Solutions
Reports on the following: burns and scalds; choking and suffocation; car seats, booster seats, and seat belts; drowning; falls; fire; home; guns; high-risk children; in and around cars; motor vehicles or cars; pedestrian;

playground; poison; rural safety; school; sport and recreation; toy; wheel; bicycling and skating. http://www.usa.safekids.org/tier3_cd_2c. cfm?content_item_id=25251&folder_id=540.

Changes in Injury and Mortality in a Twenty-Year Period
Safe Kids USA report: *Trends in Unintentional Childhood Injury: Mortality and Parental Views on Childhood Safety*, April 2008.

Population Breakdown of Children
U.S. Census Bureau
Children characteristics data set
Households and families data set
2006–2008 American Community Survey
http://factfinder.census.gov/servlet/STTable?_bm=y&-geo_id=01000US&-qr_name=ACS_2008_3YR_G00_S0901&ds_name=ACS_2008_3YR_G00_.

Accidental Injury Cost Statistics
Safe Kids USA and Safe Kids Worldwide, by topic.

Kidnapping and Missing Children
The Second National Incidence Studies of Missing, Abducted, Runaway, and Thrownaway Children (NISMART–2), U.S. Department of Justice, Office of Justice Programs, Office of Juvenile Justice and Delinquency Prevention. http://ojjdp.ncjrs.gov/publications/PubResults.asp. http://www.ncjrs.gov/html/ojjdp/nismart/02/ns4.html.

The AMBER Advocate, vol. 3, no. 4 (January 2010).

Child Overall Health and School Attendance
Bloom B., R. A. Cohen, and G. Freeman. Summary Health Statistics for U.S. Children: National Health Interview Survey, 2008. *Vital Health Statistics*, vol. 10, no. 244 (2009).

Drugs
Johnston, Lloyd D., Patrick M. O'Malley, Jerald G. Bachman, and John E. Schulenberg. *Monitoring the Future: National Survey Results on Drug Use, 1975–2008*. Vol. 1: *Secondary School Students*. Ann Arbor, MI: University of Michigan.

National Institute on Drug Abuse
6001 Executive Boulevard
Bethesda, Maryland 20892

U.S. Department of Health and Human Services. http://monitoringthe future.org/pubs/monographs/vol1_2008.pdf.

National Institute on Drug Abuse (NIDA)
InfoFacts: High School and Youth Trends. http://www.drugabuse.gov/infofacts/ HSYouthTrends.html.

Poisons
Bronstein, Alvin C., Daniel A. Spyker, Louis R. Cantilena, Jody L. Green, Barry H. Rumack, and Stuart E. Heard. 2007 Annual Report of the American Association of Poison Control Centers' National Poison Data System. *Clinical Toxicology*, vol. 46 (2008): 927–1057.

——2008 Annual Report of the American Association of Poison Control Centers' National Poison Data System. *Clinical Toxicology*, vol. 47 (2009): 911–1084.

Fear and Anxiety
Blanchard, Robert J., D. Caroline Blanchard, David Nutt, and Guy Griebel, eds. *Handbook of Anxiety and Fear*. Philadelphia: Elsevier Science & Technology Books, 2008.
Ledoux, Joseph. *The Emotional Brain: The Mysterious Underpinnings of Emotional Life*. New York: Simon & Schuster.

High School Completion
Forum on Child and Family Statistics, America's Children: Key National Indicators of Well-Being. http://www.childstats.gov/americas children/glance.asp.

Income Comparison
DeNavas-Walt, Carmen, Bernadette D. Proctor, and Cheryl Hill Lee. *Income, Poverty, and Health Insurance Coverage in the United States: 2005*. Washington, DC: U.S. Government Printing Office, 2006.

Sources by Chapter

Chapter 2. Worry Crazy Makers

Pandemic statistics: *BSE Cases in North America, by Year and Country of Death, 1993–2008*. Centers for Disease Control and Prevention, Department of Health and Human Services. 2008. http://www.cdc.gov/ncidod/dvrd/bse/images/bse_cases_namerica_2008.gif.

SARS: World Health Organization (WHO), Epidemic and Pandemic Alert and Response (EPR).

Lead toxicity: *Lead in Chocolate: The Impact on Children's Health*. American Environmental Safety Institute. May 7, 2002. http://www.fda.gov/ohrms/dockets/dailys/02/May02/050802/02p-0211cp.pdf.

Intelligence Group Reports: http://www.youthintelligence.com/.

The Mom Intelligence Survey, the Mom Intelligence Report, the Cassandra Report.

Siegel, Mark. *False Alarm: The Truth about the Epidemic of Fear*. Hoboken, NJ: John Wiley & Sons, 2005.

Glassner, Barry. *The Culture of Fear: Why Americans Are Afraid of the Wrong Things*. New York: Basic Books, 1999.

Chiricos, T., S. Eschholz, and M. Gertz. *Crime, news and fear of crime: Toward an Identification of Audience Effects*. Berkeley, CA: University of California Press, 1999.

Bikhchandani, Sushil, David, Hershliefer, and Ivo Welsh. A Theory of Fads, Fashion, Custom and Cultural Change as Informational Cascades. *Journal of Political Economy*, vol. 100, no. 5 (October 1992): 992–1026.

U.S. Consumer Product Safety Commission. *Window Covering Safety Council Recalls to Repair All Roman and Roll-Up Blinds Due to Risk of Strangulation*. December 15, 2009. http://www.cpsc.gov/cpscpub/prerel/prhtml10/10073.html.

Chapter 3. Why Worry Is Dangerous:
The Science of the Fear Epidemic
Forum on Child and Family Statistics: http://www.childstats.gov/americaschildren/glance.asp.

U.S. Census Bureau
Children characteristics data set
Households and families data set
2006–2008 American Community Survey

http://factfinder.census.gov/servlet/STTable?_bm=y&-geo_id=01000US&-qr_name=ACS_2008_3YR_G00_S0901&ds_name=ACS_2008_3YR_G00_.

Schaefer-Wilson, Jamie. *The Consumer Reports Guide to Childproofing and Safety: Tips to Protect your Baby and Child from Injury at Home and on the Go.* Consumer Reports: May 13, 2008.

Lok8u GPS tracker/finder for children: http://www.lok8u.com/us/.

Blanchard, Robert J., D. Caroline Blanchard, David Nutt, and Guy Griebel, eds. *Handbook of Anxiety and Fear.* Philadelphia: Elsevier Science & Technology Books, 2008.

Ledoux, Joseph. *The Emotional Brain: The Mysterious Underpinnings of Emotional Life.* New York: Simon & Schuster.

Seligman, M.E.P., and S.F. Maier. Failure to Escape Traumatic Shock. *Journal of Experimental Psychology*, vol. 74 (1967): 1–9.
Weiner, B. *An Attributional Theory of Motivation and Emotion.* New York: Springer-Verlag, 1986.

Bandura A. *Social Foundations of Thought and Action: A Social Cognitive Theory.* Englewood Cliffs, NJ: Prentice-Hall, 1986.

Chapter 4. Myths Exposed: Parents' Top Worries
Versus Children's Real Dangers
Stickler, Gunnar B., Margery Salter, Daniel D. Broughton, and Anthony Alario. Parents' Worries About Children Compared to Actual Risks. *Clinical Pediatrics*, vol. 30 (1991): 522–528.

Paranoid Parents Focus Group Surveys, conducted 2006–2009.

All TV stations called and interviewed by Devon Calonge for Paranoid Parents.

The Second National Incidence Studies of Missing, Abducted, Runaway, and Thrownaway Children (NISMART–2), U.S. Department of Justice, Office of Justice Programs, Office of Juvenile Justice and Delinquency Prevention: http://ojjdp.ncjrs.gov/publications/PubResults.asp.

Finkelhor, David, Heather Hammer, Andrea J. Sedlak, National Incidence Study of Missing, Abducted, Runaway and Thrownaway Children in America (NISMART 1) *(1990)*. http://www.ncjrs.gov/html/ojjdp/nismart/02/ns4.html.

The AMBER Advocate, vol. 3, no. 4 (January 2010).

The National Highway Traffic Safety Administration. Traffic Safety Facts, 2007 data: http://www-nrd.nhtsa.dot.gov/Pubs/811116.PDF.

Vossekuil, B., R. Fein, M. Reddy, R. Borum, and W. Modzeleski. Threat Assessment In Schools: A Guide to Managing Threatening Situations and to Creating Safe School Climates. Washington, DC: U.S. Government Printing Office, 2002.

Snyder, Howard N., and Melissa Sickmund. *Juvenile Offenders and Victims: 2006 National Report*. Washington, DC: U.S. Department of Justice, Office of Justice Programs, Office of Juvenile Justice and Delinquency Prevention, 2006.
National Center for Juvenile Justice
3700 S. Water Street, Suite 200
Pittsburgh, PA 15203-2363

National MCH Center for Child Death Review: http://www.childdeathreview.org/home.htm.

National Safety Council, *Injury Facts Book*, 2010. National Safety Council estimates are based on data from the National Center for Health Statistics and the U.S. Census Bureau. Deaths are classified on the basis of the tenth revision of the World Health Organization's *The International Classification of Diseases*.

Suicide, injury, deaths, and rates per 100,000, all races, both sexes, ages 15–19. http://webappa.cdc.gov/cgi-bin/broker.exe.

American Association of Suicidology.
5221 Wisconsin Avenue, NW,
Washington, DC 2001
Phone: (202) 237-2280

Johnston, Lloyd D., Patrick M. O'Malley, Jerald G. Bachman, and John E. Schulenberg. *Monitoring the Future: National Survey Results on Drug Use, 1975–2008*. Vol. 1: *Secondary School Students*. Ann Arbor, MI: University of Michigan.

National Institute on Drug Abuse
6001 Executive Boulevard
Bethesda, Maryland 20892

U.S. Department of Health and Human Services. http://monitoringthefuture.org/pubs/monographs/vol1_2008.pdf.

National Institute on Drug Abuse (NIDA)

InfoFacts: High School and Youth Trends http://www.drugabuse.gov/infofacts/HSYouthTrends.html.

Dubner, Stephen, and Steven Levitt. *Freakonomics: A Rogue Economist Explores the Hidden Side of Everything*. New York: William Morrow, 2005.

Vaccines:

Measles: http://www.cdc.gov/vaccines/vpd-vac/measles/faqs-dis-vac-risks.htm.

Rubella: http://www.immunizationinfo.org/vaccineInfo/vaccine_detail.cfv?id=24.

Measles worldwide: http://www.who.int/mediacentre/news/releases/2009/measles_mdg_20091203/en/).

Grant, Andrew. Vaccine Phobia Becomes a Public-Health Threat. *Discover* magazine, January/February, 2009.

Weighted Percentage of Students Reported Being Bullied During the Current Term: Bullying Behaviors Among U.S. Youth. *Journal of the*

American Medical Association, vol. 285 (2001): 2094-2100.

National SAFE KIDS Campaign. As above.

American Academy of Pediatrics. National Headquarters: The American Academy of Pediatrics, 141 Northwest Point Boulevard, Elk Grove Village, IL 60007-1098 USA, tel. 847/434-4000

Bronstein, Alvin C., Daniel A. Spyker, Louis R. Cantilena, Jody L. Green, Barry H. Rumack, and Stuart E. Heard. 2007 Annual Report of the American Association of Poison Control Centers' National Poison Data System. *Clinical Toxicology*, vol. 46 (2008): 927–1057.

———2008 Annual Report of the American Association of Poison Control Centers' National Poison Data System. *Clinical Toxicology*, vol. 47 (2009): 911–1084.

Chapter 5. Age-Group Essentials: Overview
Burns, Marilyn. *Math: Facing an American Phobia.* Sausalito, CA: Math Solutions, 1998.

Chapter 6. Infants
[General notes]

Chapter 7. Toddlers
List of poisons, *Clinical Toxicology*, vol. 47 (2009), 911–1084.

Bronstein, Alvin C., Daniel A. Spyker, Louis R. Cantilena, Jody L. Green, Barry H. Rumack, and Stuart E. Heard. 2007 Annual Report of the American Association of Poison Control Centers' National Poison Data System. *Clinical Toxicology*, vol. 46 (2008): 927–1057.

Bronstein, Alvin C., Daniel A. Spyker, Louis R. Cantilena, Jody L. Green, Barry H. Rumack, and Sandra L. Giffin. 2008 Annual Report of the American Association of Poison Control Centers' National Poison Data System. *Clinical Toxicology*, vol. 47 (2009): 911–1084.

American Academy of Pediatrics. Shopping Cart–Related Injuries to Children. *Pediatrics*, August 2006. http://www.pediatrics.org/cgi/doi/10.1542/peds.2006-1215 and http://www.pediatrics.org/cgi/doi/10.1542/peds.2006-1216.

Shark attacks: http://www.flmnh.ufl.edu/fish/Sharks/statistics/statsw.htm.

Glanz, Karen, Mona Saraiya, and Howell Wechsler. *Guidelines for*

School Programs to Prevent Skin Cancer. http://www.cdc.gov/mmwr/preview/ mmwrhtml/rr5104a1.htm.

Stern, R. S., M. C. Weinstein, and S. G. Baker. Risk Reduction for Nonmelanoma Skin Cancer with Childhood Sunscreen Use. *Archives of Dermatology*, vol. 122 (1986): 537–545.

Williams, M. L., and R. Pennella. Melanoma, Melanocytic Nevi, and Other Melanoma Risk Factors in Children. *Journal of Pediatrics*, vol. 124 (1994): 833–845.

Sayre, R.M., N. Kollias, R. D. Ley, and A.H. Baqer. Changing the Risk Spectrum of Injury and the Performance of Sunscreen Products Throughout the Day. *Photodermatology, Photoimmunology, and Photomedicine*, vol. 10 (1994): 148–153.

Dr. Nedrow Calonge, chief medical officer of Colorado. Interview, 2009.

Toy recalls: Wendy Bassy, CEO of Claytronics, Golden, Colorado.

Safe Kids Worldwide. *Facts About Children Injured by Toys.* http://www.usa.safekids.org/tier3_cd.cfm?folder_id=540&content_it em_id=1212.

National Vital Statistics System, National Center for Health Statistics, CDC.

Chapter 8. Elementary School

Table: National Vital Statistics System, National Center for Health Statistics, CDC.

Miracle, Andrew W., and C. Roger Rees. More Focus Needed on Academics than on Athletics. *Lessons of the Locker Room*, 1994. http://www.humanismbyjoe.com/academics_not_athletics.htm.

Boys versus girls: CDC.

The Oprah Winfrey Show, April 11, 2006.

Interview, Dr. Trish Champion, Quest program director, Belleview, Cherry Creek School District, Greenwood Village, Colorado.

Forum on Child and Family Statistics http://www.childstats.gov/americaschildren/glance.asp.

Virginia National Safety Council, Research and Statistical Services Group. *Fixed-Site Amusement Ride Injury Survey: 2007 Update.* Prepared for International Association of Amusement Parks and Attractions. Alexandria, VA: 2008.

Halloween candy:

The Denver Police: http://lifehacker.com/134056/halloween-candy-safety-tips 2005.

1970 case: http://recipes.howstuffworks.com/menus/candy-tampering.htm.

Ronald Clark O'Bryan case: http://www.halloween-website.com/poison.htm.

Chapter 9. Middle School

Table: National Vital Statistics System, National Center for Health Statistics, CDC.

TV "jet lag": http://www.manchestereveningnews.co.uk/news/health/s/176/176353_tv_stunts_kids_brain_growth.html.

Sigman, Aric. *Remotely Controlled: How Television Is Damaging Our Lives.* London: Ebury Press, 2007.

Berzins, Lisa. Dying to Be Thin: the Prevention of Eating Disorders and the Role of Federal Policy. APA co-sponsored congressional briefing. USA. 11/1997. American Psychological Association. http://www.apa.org.

Anorexia Nervosa and Related Eating Disorders: http://www.anred.com/stats.html.

The Alliance for Eating Disorders Awareness, *Eating Disorders Girl Power!* a public education program of the US Department of Health and Human Services. "Eating Disorders 101 Guide: A Summary of Issues," Statistics and www.eatingdisorderinfo.org/Resources/EatingDisorders Statistics.aspx.

Naomi Wolf, Dying to Be Thin. Congressional briefing. As above. Sports injury comparisons:

Pediatrics, vol. 117, no. 1 (January 2006): 122–129.

Pediatrics, vol. 114, no. 6 (December 2004): 661-666.

Skating: www.active.com/story.chm?story_id-12729&category=wintersports &num=0.

Skiing: National Ski Areas Association, Facts About Skiing and Snowboarding, 2006. http://www.nsaa.org/nsaa/press/0506/facts-about-skiing-and-snowboarding.asp.

Sledding: Safe Kids Worldwide. Facts About Injuries to Childhood Recreational Activities, 2000.

Snowboarding: Safe Kids Worldwide. Facts About Injuries to Childhood Recreational Activities, 2003.

National Ski Areas Association. Facts About Skiing/Snowboarding Safety. March 2006. http://www.nsaa.org/nsaa/press/0506/facts-about-skiing-and-snowboarding.asp

Snowmobiles: Safe Kids Worldwide. Facts About Injuries to Childhood Recreational Activities, 2003.

Chapter 10. High School
Table: National Vital Statistics System, National Center for Health Statistics, CDC.
Rosso, I. M., A. D. Young, L. A. Femia, and D. A. Yurgelun-Todd. Cognitive and Emotional Components of Frontal Lobe Functioning in Childhood and Adolescence. *Annals of the New York Academy of Sciences*, vol. 1021 (2004): 355–362.

Yurgelun-Todd, D. A., and W.D.S. Killgore. Fear-Related Activity in the Prefrontal Cortex Increases with Age During Adolescence: A Preliminary fMRI Study. *Neuroscience Letters*, vol. 406 (2006), 194–199.

Motor vehicle data and drinking and driving per month: CDC 2006.

Snyder, Howard N., and Melissa Sickmund. *Juvenile Offenders and Victims: 2006 National Report*. Washington, DC: U.S. Department

of Justice, Office of Justice Programs, Office of Juvenile Justice and
Delinquency Prevention, 2006.

National Center for Juvenile Justice
3700 S. Water Street, Suite 200
Pittsburgh, PA 15203-2363

Chapter 11. College
Table: National Vital Statistics System, National Center for Health
Statistics, CDC.

Safe Kids USA report: *Trends in Unintentional Childhood Injury
Mortality and Parental Views on Childhood Safety*, April 2008.

Titanic passengers: http://www.encyclopedia-titanica.org/titanic-survivor/
marjorie-collyer.html and http://www.encyclopedia-titanica.org/
titanic-survivor/robert-douglas-spedden.html.

Safe Kids USA. *Preventing Accidental Injury: Injury Facts*.

Child abuse and neglect:

Ching-Tung, Wang, and John Holton. *Economic Impact Study*. Chicago,
IL: Prevent Child Abuse America, 2007.

The Second National Incidence Studies of Missing, Abducted,
Runaway, and Thrownaway Children (NISMART–2), U.S.
Department of Justice, Office of Justice Programs, Office of Juvenile
Justice and Delinquency Prevention. http://ojjdp.ncjrs.gov/publications/
PubResults.asp.

http://www.ncjrs.gov/html/ojjdp/nismart/02/ns4.html.

Products

Paranoid Parents, created by *Paranoid Parents Guide* author Christie Barnes, brings you "stop worrying" kits as originally sold exclusively at UncommonGoods and now available at www.paranoidparentshop.com.

Parent Cue Cards. Flash cards for parents to remove the stress and worry when parenting gets a little tough. They are sold in a handy small tin to fit in your purse or pocket. All Parent Cue Card kits: $12.95.

Tantrum Tamers. For the toy store tantrum, restaurant meltdown, or surviving theme park line purgatory—learning games for tense moments.

Facts of Life for Five Year Olds. The appropriate answers to those awkward questions, before your child brings home the playground X-rated version.

Stop Worrying Sanity Cards. For parents who have ever worried and hoped to get back to the cool people you once were and have fun with your kids again. Facts and advice to put worry into perspective.

Self Esteem Kits. Self-esteem is a top concern for parents in Paranoid Parent focus surveys. Children should not receive extravagant rewards for the "nonnegotiables" of life. These kits come with buttons, information cards, reward ribbons, a shoe widget, and a zipper pull. All Self-Esteem kits: $12.95.

Kindergarten Milestones. Appropriate rewards for the accomplishments "pre-Ks" need to attempt before and during kindergarten.

Swimming Essentials. Motivating rewards for the important swimming skills needed to make your child "water safe."

Chores. Encouragement, not bribes, for children so they can follow through on chores that are a fact of life.

Must Do's With Your Kids. Instead of a toy from the zoo or a souvenir, button rewards to commemorate fun activities your kids can do with you.

Careers "Get Inspired." Get children to pretend to be Leonardo Da Vinci, Einstein, or Shakespeare or many other professions to expand their talents.

Allergy Button Kits. Included are vivid picture allergy buttons, a shoe widget, and zipper pull to make a child's allergy visible when an allergy bracelet or necklace would go unnoticed. Available separately for nut, egg, gluten, and bee sting allergies. Each Allergy kit: $9.95.

Find these and other Paranoid Parent Stop Worrying products at www.paranoidparentshop.com.

Index

abuse, 39, 61–63, 65
  risk and prevention, 62–63
airports, 15, 33–34
AMBER alerts (*see also* kidnapping),
  42–44
American Academy of Pediatrics, 112,
  132
anthrax, 13
apnea monitors, 113
attention deficit/hyperactivity disorder,
  124
author's life, 4–5
  Disney vacation, 229–230
  house fire, 80–82
  husband's death, 4–5
  moving to Colorado, 5
  shop, 8–9
  raising kids, 9, 46–47
autism (*see also* vaccines), 18
avalanches, 61

baby baths (*see also* drowning), 112, 115
baby carrier, 112
baby gates, 114
baby safety products, 111–113
Balanchine, George, 122
balloons (*see* suffocation)
baseball (*see also* sports), 151
Bassy, Wendy, 137
bicycles, 24, 39, 95–97
  bike helmets, 95, 215
  prevalence of accidents, 95
  prevention of accidents, 97
bookshelves, 114
booster seats (*see* car accidents)
boys, 7, 49–50, 164–166
  drowning, 74–75
  fire, 79–80, 83
  suicide, 66–68
breathalyzers, 195
Brownies, 220–221
bullying, 38, 88–95
  bullied parents, 216–218
  cyberbullying, 88–89
  dealing with bullying, 92–94
  defined, 89–90
  prevention, 94–95
  profile of the bullied child, 90–91
  profile of the bully, 91–92

calcium, 124
calling 911, 83
Calonge, Ned, 135
Cambridge University, 195–196
camping, 133, 221
car accidents, 39, 215
  booster seats, 50
  car seats, 48–50
  drunk driving, 19, 49
  high school students, 49–50, 184,
    186–188
  prevalence, 46
  seat belts, 46–48
  texting while driving, 187–188
car seats (*see also* car accidents), 19,
  48–50, 112, 115, 215
cell phones, 6
Centers for Disease Control (CDC), 7,
  47, 55, 60, 151, 235
cheerleading (*see also* sports), 151
childproofing, 130
Chinese toys, 137–138
Christmas tree ornaments, 141
cocaine, 70
code words, 66, 211–212
college, 34, 191–197
  graduating, 195
  sports scholarships, 147, 149
Columbine, 50, 68
Consumer Product Safety Commission,
  236
Consumer Reports, 112, 113, 138
consumer safety seals, 116–119
cost of accidents, 213–214
crib safety, 115
crib death and bedding, 87–88, 112,
  115
crime rate, 200
Cub Scouts, 220
Culture of Fear, The, 17
cyberbullying (*see* bullying)
Dawsy, Jeff, 43
death statistics by age, 107–108, 200
  college students, 192
  elementary school children, 144
  high school students, 184
  middle school students, 174
  toddlers, 122
dehydration, 166

depression, 34
detergent, 115
Devil Wears Prada, The, 176–177
diapers, 24, 155
DiCaprio, Leonardo, 209
Discover, 78–79
Disney (*see also* theme parks), 61
divorce, 85–86
dolls, 6
door bouncers, 112, 115
drowning, 39, 72–75
    bath seats, 73–74, 115
    bathtubs, 73
    life jackets, 73
    pool toys, 74
    preventing, 72–73
drugs, 38, 39, 69–72
    prevention, 71–72
    real drug use rates, 69–70
drunk driving (*see also* car accidents),
    19, 186–188
Dubner, Stephen, 72

eating disorders, 175–178
ecstasy, 70
elementary school children
    mortality, 144
    sports injuries, 145–146
Extreme Makeover, 30

*False Alarm: The Truth About the
    Epidemic of Fear*, 17
fear as a marketing tool, 11–12
fight-or-flight instinct, 26–27
fire, 33, 39, 79–83
    prevention, 80, 82–83
Five-Minute Worry Test, 2
flashing, 193–194
floods, 101
flu, 108
Food and Drug Administration (FDA),
    7, 14
Freakonomics, 72

gangs, 39
girls, 6, 164–166
    eating disorders, 176–178
    suicide, 66–68
Glassner, Barry, 17

Good Housekeeping Seal of Approval,
    117
GPS child tracking devices, 25,
    188–189
Grant, Hugh, 4
gun violence, 57, 201
gymnastics (*see also* sports), 151

H1N1 vaccine, 20
Halloween candy, 168–171
head injuries, 33, 130–132
helmets (*see* bicycles)
heroin, 70
high chairs, 114
high school, 183–190
    car accidents, 184
    drop-out rate, 155–156
    spying on, 188–190
hockey, 151–152
home as a theme park, 30, 159–160
homicide, 39
    causes, 56
    prevalence, 55
Horton, Richard, 77
hot water controllers, 115
hugging, 68

ice skating (*see also* sports), 151–152
immunity, 108–109
infant mortality rate, 111–112
information cascade theory, 18–19
ink cartridges, 130
in-line skating (*see also* sports), 151
Intelligence Group, 15
Internet access, 68
Ipsas MORI, 38

jewelry, 139
jogging strollers, 8, 114–115

kidnapping, 38, 40, 65
    AMBER Alerts, 42–44
    prevalence, 40–42, 44–45
    prevention, 45–46
kitchen dangers, 116

latchkey kids, 63
learned helplessness, 31–34
Leela, 4
Levitt, Steven, 72

lightning, 61, 101–102
London, 5, 48–49

mad cow disease, 13
magnesium, 124
magnets, 140
makeup, 139
malls, 21, 41, 52
marijuana, 70
Mattel, 137
Mayo Clinic, 40
McCann, Madeleine, 12
measles, 19, 75–76
media sensationalism, 12–14, 34,
    199–200
meerkat moms, 6
    kidnapping, 40
methamphetamines, 70
Mickey Mouse, 61
middle school years, 173–182
missingchild.wordpress.com, 40
Mom Intelligence Survey, 15
mothballs, 130
mumps, 19, 75

nagging, 33, 207–208
National Center for Missing and
    Exploited Children (see also
    kidnapping), 41–42
National Electronic Injury Surveillance
    System, 236
National Highway Traffic Safety
    Administration, 47–48
natural disasters, 38, 101–102
Netherlands, 176
Notting Hill, 4
nursery school, 122

Ohio State University, 131
omega-3 fatty acides, 125–126
organic foods, 125
Oxford University, 195–196

pacifiers, 112
Paranoid Parents
    bumper stickers, 9, 35–36
    Denver poll, 38
    focus groups, 3
    Paranoid Parent Stop Worrying
        Shoppe, 7–9

parenting mistakes, 28–30, 106–107,
    222–225
pedophiles, 20, 33
Pennington, Ty, 30
perfume, 139
plastic, 14, 24
    baby products, 115
    bags (see suffocation)
    toys, 137–138
playground injuries, 157–159
playing in the yard, 38, 84–86
poisoning, 39, 99–100
    household poisons, 99
    prevention, 100
    statistics by age and type of poison,
        127–129
polio, 19
post-traumatic stress disorder, 59
poverty, 56, 71, 80
pregnancy manuals, 116–117
prescription drugs, 71

reading to kids, 156–157
Red Cross, 176
rewarding good behavior, 163–164
Robert, Julia, 4
rubella, 75–76
Ryan, Meg, 8, 37

SafeKids, 215, 236
SARS, 13
school buses, 38, 97–98
    safety record, 97
school drop-off, 84–85
school snipers, 12, 16, 20, 33, 38,
    50–55
    prevalence, 52
    prevention, 54–55
    sniper proofing schools, 52–54
schools, picking, 153–155
seat belts (see car accidents)
sexting, 194
sexual activity, 20
    and college, 196–197
shampoo, 115
shark attack, 16, 133–134
shopping carts, 130–133
shower curtains, 14
Siegel, Marc, 17
skateboarding, 178–179

skiing, 180–182
sledding, 181
sleep sack, 115
Sleepless in Seattle, 37
smoke alarms (*see also* fire), 80, 83, 215
snowboarding, 181–182
soap, 115
soft drinks, 125
spoiling kids, 159–163
sports, 24, 145–153, 215
    chances of going pro, 146–147
    extreme sports, 178–179
    preventing injuries, 150–153
    scholarships, 147, 149
    snowboarding, 181–182
    sportsmanship, 149
    when to start, 147–148
    winter sports, 180–182
Stabinger, Karen, 194
statistics, interpreting, 233–236
stranger danger, 38, 62, 64–66
    reducing risk, 65–66
strokes, 102–103
strollers, 112, 114–115
suffocation, 39, 86–88
    balloons, 86–87, 139–140
sugar, 123–126
    addiction, 126
    decreasing intake, 124–125
suicide, 6–7, 39, 66–69
    prevalence, 67
sun exposure, 134–136
sunscreen, 134–136
swine flu, 24
swing sets, 158

television, 174–175
terrorism, 5, 13, 38
    London train bombings, 58–59
    prevalence, 60–61
    September 11, 2001, 16, 59–60, 211

theme parks, 16, 20, 133, 166–168
    rides, 167
Time magazine, 38
Titanic: The Artifact Exhibition, 209–210
toddlers
    annual causes of death, 121
    early education, 122–123
    sugar, 123–126
tornadoes, 101
toys, 137–141
    Chinese toys, 137–138
    dangerous toys, 139–140
    recalls, 139
    riding toys, 140
trampolines, 222
U.S. Consumer Product Safety Commission, 114, 131
U.S. Justice Department, 42

vacations, 133–134, 206
vaccines, 18–19, 38, 75–79
    benefits, 75–76
    links with autism, 76–78
video games, 24
Virginia Tech, 50

walkers, 115
walking helmets, 6
West Nile virus, 13
window blinds, 20, 87, 114
windows, 114–115
Winslet, Kate, 209
wooden toys, 137–138
World Health Organization (WHO), 7, 76
worrying
    addiction, 28, 201–212
    effect on children, 30–31
    ineffectiveness, 22, 28–29
    physical manifestation, 27–28
    prevalence, 3

You've Got Mail, 8, 9